Suicide

The Philosophical Dimensions

GW00775941

Suicide

The Philosophical Dimensions

Michael Cholbi

BROADVIEWGUIDES to PHILOSOPHY

Library and Archives Canada Cataloguing in Publication

Cholbi, Michael
  Suicide : the philosophical dimensions / by Michael Cholbi.

(Broadview guides to philosophy)
Includes bibliographical references and index.
ISBN 978-1-55111-905-2

  1. Suicide. 2. Suicide—Philosophy. I. Title II. Series: Broadview guides to philosophy

HV6545.C46 2011   362.28'01   C2011-903214-7

Broadview Press is an independent, international publishing house, incorporated in 1985.

We welcome comments and suggestions regarding any aspect of our publications—please feel free to contact us at the addresses below or at broadview@broadviewpress.com.

North America
PO Box 1243, Peterborough, Ontario, Canada K9J 7H5
2215 Kenmore Ave., Buffalo, New York, USA 14207
Tel: (705) 743-8990; Fax: (705) 743-8353
email: customerservice@broadviewpress.com

UK, Europe, Central Asia, Middle East, Africa, India, and Southeast Asia
Eurospan Group, 3 Henrietta St., London WC2E 8LU, United Kingdom
Tel: 44 (0) 1767 604972; Fax: 44 (0) 1767 601640
email: eurospan@turpin-distribution.com

Australia and New Zealand
NewSouth Books
c/o TL Distribution, 15-23 Helles Ave., Moorebank, NSW, Australia 2170
Tel: (02) 8778 9999; Fax: (02) 8778 9944
email: orders@tldistribution.com.au

www.broadviewpress.com

Copy-edited by Martin Boyne

This book is printed on paper containing 100% post-consumer fibre.

Design and composition by George Kirkpatrick

PRINTED IN CANADA

Contents

Acknowledgements

THIS BOOK IS THE culmination of over a decade of philosophical inquiry into suicide. The philosophical literature on suicide is voluminous, but philosophers have tended to address suicide piecemeal, addressing philosophical questions about suicide in isolation from one another. Here I have striven to work both analytically and synthetically, so that while each chapter can be read profitably on its own, the book nevertheless represents a sustained investigation into the nature and ethics of suicide. I make no pretense of having issued "the last word" on any of the philosophical questions I discuss here. My hope is that this book will serve instead as a provocative "first word" on these questions and thereby stimulate further interest in, and research about, them.

In writing this book, I have incurred many debts. My interest in philosophical questions surrounding suicide can be traced to a graduate seminar at the University of Virginia on Kant's ethics, where John Marshall encouraged me to sympathetically engage Kant's position on suicide. Over the years, many philosophers have provided input on the ideas and arguments contained herein, and I wish to single out Chris Naticchia, John Davis, and Rivka Weinberg for special gratitude. I have also profited immeasurably from numerous discussions about suicide with my departmental colleague David Adams. The staff at Broadview Press have patiently and professionally seen this book to fruition. Ryan Chynces in particular deserves my gratitude for approaching me about the possibility of this book in 2006.

Work on this project was also supported by California State Polytechnic University, Pomona. The university provided me with a Research, Scholarship, and Creative Activities (RSCA) grant in 2007 and granted me a faculty sabbatical in 2009, enabling me to make progress on this book at key junctures in its development.

Introduction

There is but one truly serious philosophical problem and that is suicide.[1]

PHILOSOPHERS HAVE A WELL-DESERVED reputation for transforming the ordinary into the extraordinary—for taking facets of daily life and, through relentlessly applying their powers of reason and argument, making these into challenging and complex intellectual problems. That the world perceived by the senses is an illusion, that time is unreal, that motion and change are impossible—philosophers are the ones who deserve credit (or blame) for compelling us to take such theses seriously.

Yet there are other features of human existence that are sufficiently strange and puzzling on their own that we hardly need philosophers' help to see them as serious or compelling. Suicide is one such problem. On the one hand, suicide is hardly unknown, having been cataloged by anthropologists in a wide range of cultures across time and space, and it remains commonplace in modern society. A death by suicide occurs every forty seconds, suicide is among the top ten causes of death in the world, and the majority of adults report knowing someone who has at least thought about suicide. Indeed, the number

---

1   Albert Camus, *The Myth of Sisyphus and Other Essays*, trans. J. O'Brien (New York: Vintage, 1991), p. 3.

of people who try suicide exceeds the number who die by suicide by a ratio of a hundred to one. Yet on the other hand, viewed on a different scale, the act of taking one's own life is comparatively rare. Around one million people worldwide end their lives each year in an act of suicide, a small fraction of the tens of millions who die from other causes.[1]

But it is not only the relative infrequency of suicide that makes it strange or puzzling. From the perspective of an outsider observing suicidal behavior, understanding the motivations behind suicide can also be challenging. There seem to be two goals that motivate almost all human behavior. First, we spend much of our lives attending to our basic survival needs, seeking out food and shelter and avoiding illness and injury. When a person takes her own life, she thus seems to be acting in opposition to the fundamental biological imperative of survival. Second, as complex creatures we seek not only survival but also that elusive state of well-being or contentment we call *happiness*. Suicidal individuals appear to be giving up on pursuing that objective as well, choosing death over any future chance at happiness. Part of the reason that suicide puzzles us is that it does not fit comfortably into either category of motivation. The fact of suicide makes it conceivable, yet it is the most inconceivable of human acts.

This challenge of simply understanding why suicide happens may explain the striking diversity of attitudes toward suicide throughout the history of human culture. Suicide inspires fear, rage, sorrow, sympathy, curiosity, and moral disgust. Some strongly religious societies have seen suicide as an offense against God, others as according with God's wishes or commands. The ancient Stoic philosophers thought of suicide as a lucid and rational response to the misery or futility of the human condition, whereas other cultures have thought of suicide as sure evidence of madness or delirium. In some societies, suicide has been condemned as disruptive of social order and contrary to the inherent value of human life, whereas other cultures, such as the warrior culture of Japan, have seen suicide as sometimes the only honorable response to shameful events or misdeeds. And for those left behind, suicide can spark conflicting emotions as well.

Does this diversity of opinion about suicide mean that philosophy has nothing to contribute to the study or understanding of suicide? On the contrary. Where there is fundamental disagreement about some important issue

---

1   American Association of Suicidology, "National Suicide Stats and Tools," 2010 (http://www.suicidology.org/web/guest/stats-and-tools).

in human life is precisely where philosophy can make a contribution. A great deal of this disagreement could stem from our not having given suicide the kind of careful reflection in which philosophy specializes. Perhaps, then, some clarity about suicide can be achieved if suicide is placed under a philosophical lens and examined carefully. There is, of course, no guarantee that a philosophical investigation of suicide will yield unambiguous answers to our questions, but that is not something we can judge beforehand.

Philosophers have been interested in suicide since at least the time of Plato, but their attention to suicide tends to wax and wane in response to intellectual fashion or cultural trends. Recently suicide has returned to the philosophical and public policy agenda with a vengeance. The first reason for this resurgence of interest is that advances in medical technology and changes in attitudes about death and dying have brought euthanasia and physician-assisted suicide to the forefront of popular attention. Many people now believe that choosing the circumstances of one's own death is a basic moral right and that physicians should be allowed to aid their patients in the exercise of this right. Others argue that euthanasia or physician-assisted suicide fails to respect the value of human life or would be dangerous if implemented. The complexity of the philosophical issues raised by euthanasia and physician-assisted suicide make them a ripe area of philosophical research. A second reason for suicide receiving greater attention recently is the increased awareness of mental health and mental illness, especially depression. Slowly but steadily, social stigmas attaching to mental illness are lifting, especially as powerful new pharmaceutical treatments are unveiled. Naturally, this change in attitude toward mental illness should lead to a re-examination of our attitudes toward suicide, since mental illness is strongly implicated as a contributing factor to suicidal thought and behavior.

The purpose of this book is to investigate some of the central philosophical questions surrounding suicide. These questions are conceptual, metaphysical, psychological, and ethical in nature. The book is meant to be introductory and makes no claim to comprehensiveness in its treatment of the philosophical questions surrounding suicide. Instead, my hope is that readers will find the philosophical discussions in this book sufficiently stimulating that they will be inspired to consult the vast philosophical literature on suicide. To that end, I have included a brief list of suggested readings at the conclusion of each chapter. Readers can find detailed bibliographic information about the suggested readings in the bibliography.

The book is most profitably read in its entirety. However, it is also designed to be a useful reference source, either for those who wish to know about a particular philosopher's views or to investigate a particular philosophical question about suicide, or as a starting place for further reading or research.

Chapter One investigates a question that may appear pedantic at first glance but actually has many implications: how shall we define suicide? As we shall see, it is not obvious whether or not some behaviors are suicidal.

Chapter Two begins what is in many respects the core concern of the book: the ethics of suicide. This chapter describes and critically appraises the main historical arguments for the moral wrongfulness of suicide. After dividing these into religious and non-religious arguments, I first discuss the main religious arguments, including the property argument, the "life as God's gift" argument, and Aquinas's natural law argument (with particular attention paid to Hume's critique of the latter). We will then turn to the principal non-religious arguments, including the sanctity of life argument, the arguments that suicide violates duties owed to the state or to one's society, the argument that suicide violates duties owed to family or loved ones, and Kant's argument (recently revived by David Velleman) that suicide is contrary to human beings' standing as autonomous rational agents. Though I will conclude that none of these arguments establishes even a strong presumption that suicide is (in general) morally wrong, some of the non-religious arguments imply that suicide may be wrong in particular cases.

Chapter Three complements Chapter Two, as it addresses the principal arguments for the moral permissibility of suicide. These arguments appeal to self-defense, our knowledge of our own interests or well-being, our ownership of our own bodies, and our autonomy as rational beings. Here my conclusions parallel those of Chapter Two: none of these arguments is uncontroversially sound.

Chapter Four considers whether *not* taking one's own life is ever morally wrong. In other words, is there ever a duty to die? We consider here four scenarios in which, some philosophers have argued, there may be a duty to commit suicide: suicide in the service of a political or religious cause, suicide ordered by the state, suicide to remove burdens one is placing on others, and suicide to save the lives of others. I argue that if there is a duty to die, it is likely to be rare.

Chapter Five considers our moral obligations to suicidal people. More specifically, do we ever have a duty to prevent others from taking their own lives?

There I argue that although many of the measures we can take to prevent or intervene in suicide are morally benign, some of these measures are problematic because they cause serious harm to suicidal individuals or because they interfere with those individuals' liberty or autonomy.

Chapter Six examines the hotly contested ethical issue of assisted suicide. I argue that whether we have a duty to assist others in ending their lives depends both on whether the suicides in question are themselves morally permissible and on the closeness of our relationship to the suicidal individual. The chapter concludes with a discussion of whether medical professionals have a duty to assist in suicide.

In the epilogue, I investigate an issue that, while not itself a philosophical question, has clear philosophical implications: why do people commit suicide? I analyze this question in terms of the means, motive, and opportunity that individuals have to take their own lives.

I intend this book to be an introduction to, or overview of, the main philosophical issues surrounding suicide. That being said, it is an opinionated introduction. I defend the conclusions that strike me as best supported by sound reasoning and evidence. Some will be persuaded by these conclusions; others will not be. For the latter group, I hope that my arguments will be sufficiently provocative that you will be inspired to figure out where I have gone wrong. Obviously, this book can unravel only a few main strands of the large tapestry of philosophical issues that suicide raises. By its conclusion, I hope that readers will be persuaded that philosophical inquiry can shed light on many of the most important questions we have about suicide and that it raises questions of profound philosophical interest in its own right.

Further Reading

A number of sources provide good general overviews of the philosophical issues surrounding suicide. These include Cholbi (2008), Donnelly (1998), and Battin (1996) and (2005). For more historical or cultural introductions, see Minois (1999) and Alvarez (1990). Jamison (2000) is an excellent introduction to the science and psychology of suicide. The American Association of Suicidology (http://www.suicidology.org) is a pre-eminent group of scholars studying the phenomenon of suicide.

one

The Nature of Suicide

A swimmer in distress cries, "I shall drown; no one will save me!" A suicide puts it the other way: "I will drown; no one shall save me!" In relaxed speech, however, the words shall *and* will *are seldom used precisely; our ear guides us or fails to guide us, as the case may be, and we are quite likely to drown when we want to survive and survive when we want to drown.*[1]

WE BEGIN OUR INVESTIGATION of suicide with a surprisingly elusive question: just what *is* suicide?

Some Examples

Consider the following examples. As you read them, ask yourself this question: was the person's death suicide—or, put differently, was the behavior suicidal?

Skydiver: A skydiver enthusiastically jumps from an airplane and descends toward earth. However, the skydiver's parachute fails to open, and he crashes to the ground and dies.

---

1   Willliam Strunk and E.B. White, *The Elements of Style*, 3rd ed. (Boston: Allyn and Bacon, 1995), p. 58.

Despondent: A despondent man, whose past includes two previous suicide attempts, drives to a tall cliff and throws himself off.

Cutter: A young, depressed woman gashes her arm with a razor. She knows that sufficient blood loss will lead her to pass out. Lonely and desperate, she hopes that she will be found by others so that they will comfort her. She is later found unconscious but alive in her bathtub.

Shooter: A young, depressed man wants to illustrate to the girlfriend who recently broke up with him just how much distress or anguish their breakup has caused him. He hatches a plan to wound himself. He finds a loaded handgun, places it under his arm, and fires. Unexpectedly, the bullet enters his heart and kills him instantly.

Spy: A spy is captured by enemy forces and threatened with torture if she does not reveal her nation's military plans. Conscious of the importance of keeping these secrets and doubtful that she can psychologically withstand the torture without revealing the plans, the spy uses her belt to hang herself in her holding cell.

Robber: An angry criminal goes to a bank planning a holdup. He does not intend to take the bank's money, however. His plan is instead to create a hostage situation that will provoke the police into killing him. His plan succeeds: a police sniper shoots and kills the robber when the robber refuses to release a hostage held at gunpoint.

Foxhole Jumper: A soldier sees that the enemy has tossed a live grenade into his foxhole. Aware that the grenade's full detonation will kill the other members of his unit encamped in the foxhole, the soldier jumps atop the grenade to absorb the blast with his body. He is killed by the explosion.

Cancer Patient: A middle-aged woman is diagnosed with an untreatable form of cancer. After hearing her treatment options, she carefully considers whether, in light of the discomfort or pain of treatment and the possibility of extending her life, she should seek treatment. She then opts not to have her cancer treated, and her cancer kills her six months later.

Life Support: An elderly man kept alive by life support decides he no longer wants to live and instructs his physician to remove the life-support technologies. He dies within hours.

Dissident: A political dissident is sentenced to die for criticizing a totalitarian government. However, his sentence is that he must administer a lethal injection to himself or the state will forcibly kill him. The dissident chooses the former option and dies by injecting himself with a cocktail of fatal drugs.

Are Skydiver, Despondent, Cutter, Shooter, Spy, Robber, Foxhole Jumper, Cancer Patient, Life Support, and Dissident examples of suicide? Do the individuals in each example engage in suicidal behavior? For those who die, would you say that suicide is responsible for their deaths?

It may not be obvious precisely how to respond to these examples. They may well confuse you rather than clarify what suicide is. But this is the consequence of the fact that our notion of what suicide is turns out to be underdeveloped or inconsistent. The aim of this chapter is to help clarify the nature of suicide.

What Should a Definition of Suicide Capture?

Philosophers love attempting to define ordinary concepts or ideas. Such attempts often strike non-philosophers as nitpicky exercises with no larger point than to illustrate philosophers' impressive ability to make ever finer distinctions or contrive ever more elaborate examples for consideration. But in the case of suicide, figuring out the best definition or characterization of the notion is not simply an idle exercise, for there are a wide variety of attitudes or practices where it matters how we characterize suicide. For one thing, whether a person's behavior is classified as suicidal has many practical implications. Few life insurers, for example, honor policies for those who commit suicide. Suicidal behavior is sometimes a diagnostic indicator of various mental disorders, and whether someone is considered a danger to herself or others, and hence eligible to be hospitalized or institutionalized even against her will, can turn on whether an episode is categorized as a suicide attempt. Public health officials also have a strong interest in how suicide is characterized because its prevalence within the general population or within more specific populations (teens, the elderly, veterans, etc.) is often seen as a rough measure of the well-being of that population. The family members and friends of deceased individuals also have reason to care about whether an action is classified as suicide. At the very least, they have understandable desires to know the circumstances of their loved ones' deaths. Such desires are a natural outgrowth of our longing to know the inner mental lives of those we love and care about. Finally, suicide is a subject of moral concern (a concern we begin to investigate in earnest in the next chapter).

But we can hardly have an intelligible discussion about the morality of suicide—whether suicide is ever morally permissible, morally required, and so forth—unless we have some idea of what the phenomenon itself is. There is the very real risk that such discussion will run aground because the parties to the discussion simply do not share a common conception of suicide. Suppose that Matilda and Nancy disagree about the morality of suicide. Matilda believes suicide is always immoral, whereas Nancy believes some suicides are not immoral. Note, however, that Matilda and Nancy would actually be in agreement if all of the cases that Nancy believes are examples of morally permissible suicides turn out, according to Matilda's understanding of suicide, not to be suicides at all. Nancy might believe, for instance, that suicide is morally permissible if it is motivated by a concern to protect the welfare of others, but Matilda might view only self-killings motivated solely by self-interest as suicides. Clarifying the nature of suicide thus seems essential if we are to locate our own positions on the morality of suicide and identify where they diverge from others'.

An adequate characterization of suicide should aspire to meet at least two criteria. The first flows from the aforementioned fact that suicide is a morally controversial topic. As we observed, progress in thinking about the morality of suicide is impeded when we lack a clear understanding of the nature of suicide. Beyond this problem, though, progress is also impeded if our conception of suicide happens to be value-laden rather than descriptive. Let us consider an example to illustrate this problem. The English language has more than one word to designate acts whereby one person kills another. "Homicide" means exactly that: the killing of one person by another. Note that "homicide" appears to be a descriptive or value-neutral term. Its definition says nothing about whether an act of homicide is good or bad, or right or wrong. (That's why it can make sense to speak of "justifiable homicide.") In contrast, our word "murder" is usually defined as the wrongful or criminal killing of another person. This word's definition is not descriptive but value-laden. To call a killing a "murder" is to say that it was wrong, whereas to classify a killing as a "homicide" leaves an open question as to the morality of the act. Every murder is a homicide, but not every homicide is a murder. Failure to recognize when a term is value-laden can frustrate attempts to think and talk about the morality of a certain practice.

Suppose a moral opponent of abortion defends her position on the grounds that abortion is murder. Now if the abortion opponent intends her claim "abortion is murder" to refer to the *definition* of abortion, she has simply begged the question against anyone who might disagree with her. If the proper definition of abortion includes that it is an act of murder, then someone who believes that some abortions are morally permissible could not really believe that, since "abortion" has been defined as *murder* and "murder" means *a wrongful killing*. If that were the definition, then "some abortions are not murders" is contradictory, much in the same way that "some mammals are hairless" and "some triangles have four sides" are contradictory. But the disagreement between these individuals does not seem to be linguistic at heart, where one of the individuals really understands the meaning of "abortion" but the other does not. Rather, their disagreement is a moral one, about whether abortion has the further property of being morally wrong or not, and it is neither fair nor illuminating to settle the dispute by appealing to value-laden definitions such as "abortion is murder." Better instead that the parties to the dispute settle upon a descriptive characterization of abortion—something like "a surgical procedure to terminate pregnancy"—that will then permit them to have a serious ethical discussion about abortion.

I propose, then, that a suitable characterization of suicide needs to avoid these pitfalls and aspire to being descriptive rather than value-laden. This, however, is easier said than done. For it is clear that although antagonistic attitudes toward suicide have changed a great deal over time, the word "suicide" still carries strongly negative connotations in many people's minds. Most people are more likely to see the deaths of those they loathe (e.g., Hitler) as suicides than the deaths of those they admire (e.g., Jesus, who is reported to have said in John 10:17, "the Father loves Me, because I lay down My life so that I may take it again."). Similarly, our attitudes toward various policies seem to be sensitive to whether those policies are presented in terms of "suicide" or not. This is especially clear from the public debate about physician-assisted suicide. For example, in opinion polls conducted in the United States, a majority will typically support allowing doctors "to help end the lives" of patients with terminal illnesses if the patient so requests, but the margin of support shrinks when polling subjects are asked whether they support laws allowing doctors to "assist patients to commit suicide." Obviously, the word "suicide" carries significant negative overtones, since to allow doctors to end the lives of consenting patients at their request and to allow doctors to assist patients in their suicides is essentially the same thing! It is no surprise, then, that politically savvy supporters of assisted suicide tend to frame their position in terms of "death with dignity," "aid in dying," and so on. Conversely, "suicide" may also evoke sympathy that some believe is unwarranted. There has long been controversy concerning the phrase "suicide bomber," for example. Japanese *kamikaze* pilots and Muslim terrorists have long been referred to with this phrase, but some object to this usage, saying that it romanticizes such actions and overlooks the fact that their main purpose is not suicide, but homicide.

Challenging though it may be, we should nevertheless attempt to define suicide in a wholly descriptive way. Second, despite the initial difficulty involved in classifying some of the trickier examples I outlined above, an adequate characterization of suicide should make sense of the clear-cut examples on either side of the definitional boundary. Of the aforementioned examples, Skydiver is probably the most clear-cut example of behavior that is *not* suicide. The skydiver's death is accidental, for one thing, and it would be reasonable to say that death is not part of his intention at all. If the thought of dying enters his mind, it does so as something he is seeking to avoid despite his risky behavior. In contrast, Despondent looks like a clear-cut example of suicide. Ideally, our account of what suicide is will help us decide what to say about problematic examples, but any account that cannot explain the easy examples should be rejected.

In tandem, these two criteria may not point directly to a single correct characterization of suicide. However, I hope to show that they can put us in the area of such a characterization.

Suicide as Intentional Self-killing

Let's return to our initial examples and see if progress on a plausible definition of suicide might be possible. In my estimation, the most plausible definition of suicide is the following.

(S) Suicide is intentional self-killing: a person's act is suicidal if and only if the person believed that the act, or some causal consequence of that act, would make her death likely and she engaged in the behavior to intentionally bring about her death.

(S) appears to be very promising as a definition of suicide. It is descriptive rather than evaluative, making no reference to whether or not suicidal behavior is moral or immoral, justified or unjustified, rational or irrational. But how well does (S) do with respect to our second desideratum, of accounting for clear-cut examples?

(S) is an intricate definition, so to determine how successful it is in classifying various examples, we need to proceed carefully and analyze each component of (S) in turn.

"Suicide" and "suicidal"

The simplest definition of suicide is that it is self-killing, but this is a misleading definition. Some behaviors that we deem "suicidal" don't result in a person being killed; we do, after all, recognize a category of behaviors as suicide *attempts*. Hence, an adequate definition of suicide must enable us to make sense not only of deaths that are suicides but also other suicidal behaviors that do not result in death. Put differently, whatever suicide is, attempted suicides must be attempts to do *that*. This is why (S) understands suicide in terms of a certain kind of act, a suicidal act. Suicide itself is therefore an effect of some suicidal acts; that is, suicide occurs when an act in which a person intentionally kills herself actually results in death. While some contrast "attempted" suicides with "successful" suicides or "completed" suicides, I will simply speak of "suicide" to refer to acts that are suicidal and will indicate, when necessary, that the suicide resulted in death.

"Self-killing"

The notion of *self* in self-killing is tricky. In many instances of suicide, the sequence of events that leads immediately to the person's death originates outside the person. For example, consider Robber above. This is an example of what is known as "suicide by cop," where an individual commits a crime in an effort to lead law-enforcement agents to kill him. In a strict sense, Robber does not kill himself. The police kill him, and indeed, some might call such police killings justifiable *homicides*. Yet it still seems intuitively correct to say that Robber's act is suicidal. After all, he set out to create conditions in which his own death would occur. Likewise with Life Support: the man in Life Support does not remove the life support, but instead instructs his doctor to do so. Indeed, in a strict sense, neither he nor his doctor is the cause of his death. His cancer causes his death, yet this is the sort of example that is often classified as assisted suicide. So too with Foxhole Jumper: the cause of his death is the grenade thrown in the foxhole, even though its being thrown is an event he has no part in making happen. The "self" in the description of suicide as self-killing thus does not refer to the cause of a person's death in the narrow sense. Nor does it refer to a specific means of killing or of putting oneself at risk of being killed. Indeed, a wide spectrum of behaviors count as suicide, so what makes suicide what it is cannot be how the death or risk thereof is specifically caused. Regardless of whether a death or the risk thereof is (a) causally initiated by the person in question, or (b) the specific means (gunshot, drug overdose, etc.), it may be appropriate to label such behavior suicidal.

"Likely" to "bring about"

Suicide occurs not when death is a result of what one does, but when death is brought about by one's acts. Consider this example:

> **Mistaken**: A depressed man ingests all of his prescription sleeping pills in the hope that it will kill him. However, his act rests on a mistaken belief that the full bottle of sleeping pills will in fact kill him. A few hours before, the man drank a large quantity of vodka. The combination of the vodka and the sleeping pills kills him.

In Mistaken, the depressed man's act leads to his death. As we will fully appreciate later in the chapter, according to (S), the depressed man's act of taking the sleeping pills is suicidal. However, his death is not suicide, because what brings about his death is not his act of taking the pills but the chemical interaction of the pills with alcohol. His mistaken belief generates what is known as a deviant causal chain, wherein his death does not result from his suicidal act.

Puzzles may arise about how likely an act is to bring about one's death in order for it to be counted as suicidal. Do Russian-roulette players who die count as suicides, for instance? Many players will have the good fortune of firing empty chambers, but one will not. Or take chronic smokers. Most smokers know that smoking tobacco greatly increases their risk of getting fatal illnesses. Is smoking suicidal, then? We tend not to suppose so, but a case can be made that the *habit* of smoking is suicidal even if smoking any *one* cigarette is not. (This will become clearer in our later discussion of what makes an outcome intentional.) The already addicted smoker who smokes one more cigarette is not making her death much more likely than it was before, given that the risk of later death increases only minutely with each cigarette smoked. But beginning to smoke, or developing a smoking habit, greatly increases the risk of death and is suicidal to that extent.

"Intentionally"

Most philosophical definitions of suicide accept that suicide is intentional self-killing. This helps to explain our natural reactions to various examples. Contrast the examples of Robber or Despondent with examples such as Skydiver and Shooter. The latter do not appear to be examples of suicide, whereas the former do. How come? Skydiver and Shooter are most naturally thought of as accidental deaths because neither Skydiver nor Shooter's death is intentional. Skydiver assumed that he had taken effective precautions (packing his parachute correctly, etc.) to avoid death. Thus, he was in no way intending to die by jumping from the plane. Shooter is perhaps a bit more ambiguous: he seeks to elicit sympathy from his ex-girlfriend through an action that mimics death, but because of his carelessness or ignorance, that action ends up causing his own death. But even then, it was not any part of his intention to bring about his own death.

However, controversy about what renders a self-killing intentional emerges when considering examples such as Spy or Foxhole Jumper. Some would claim that these are not suicides because in these cases, the individual dies as a consequence of an act of self-killing, but death is no part of the individual's intention. In an example like Spy, Spy does not engage in the life-threatening behavior *intending* to bring about her death. Rather, her intention is to prevent the enemy from learning the crucial military secrets she fears she will divulge under torture. Hence, Spy does not engage in suicide. Likewise, Foxhole Jumper intends to save his fellow soldiers by jumping on the grenade. In all likelihood, Foxhole Jumper foresees that death will result from his jumping on the grenade, but death is not his intention.

In contrast, I believe that Spy and Foxhole Jumper are intentional self-killings and hence examples of suicide. In order to see why, we will need to examine what makes a self-killing intentional.

Let us begin with this claim:

(N1) An individual's self-killing is intentional just in case death is the intention of the act that resulted in the individual's death.

As it will turn out, I will argue that (N1) is false. For now, we should note that (N1) seems unhelpful. It defines intentional self-killing in terms of death's being an individual's intention. But what makes death the intention of someone's act? Here is an initial account of what makes death a person's intention:

(N2) Death is the intention of an act just in case being dead is the end or justifying reason for that act.

Taken together, (N1) and (N2) imply (N3):

(N3) An individual's self-killing is intentional just in case being dead is the end or justifying aim for that act.

But (N2) cannot be right. Certainly, the best way to express Spy's end or aim in hanging herself is not that she seeks to bring about her death (or the state of her being dead). Rather, she intends to die but only because doing so serves some other end she had: namely, to keep the military secrets away from her enemies. So too in several other examples we have considered: individuals are intending to die inasmuch as they act with the understanding that their actions will likely bring about their deaths, where they also believe that dying will serve some other end or aim they have (saving others' lives, relieving their own suffering, etc.). While it is possible to intend death for its own sake (someone could end her life simply from a desire to experience death or dying), in the overwhelming number of instances of suicidal behavior, a person intends to die in the sense that dying is a means to a distinct end or aim to which the person is otherwise committed. Or to put the same point slightly differently: a person's behavior is suicidal when they intend to die as the means to some other end that they also intend. If we too readily assimilate a person's intentions to her ends or aims, we actually end up showing that even the most clear-cut cases of suicide (for example, Despondent) are not suicide at all, since in those cases the person does not intend to die for the sake of dying. Hence, to identity a person's intentions with her ends could lead to the very surprising conclusion that suicide never occurs!

Thus, since (N2) is incorrect, (N3) should be rejected. Yet our criticisms of (N2) point toward a better account of death as a person's intention:

(N4) Death is the intention of an act just in case either (a) being dead is the end or justifying reason for that act, or (b) death is the individual's chosen means for achieving her end or justifying aim.

(N4), in conjunction with (N1), implies (N5):

(N5) An individual's self-killing is intentional just in case either (a) being dead is the end or justifying reason for that act, or (b) death is the individual's chosen means for achieving her end or justifying aim.

By broadening the notion of intention, (N5) represents an advance over (N3). We do tend to think of our intentions not merely in terms of our ends, but also in terms of the means we choose so as to satisfy those ends. We eat in order to satisfy our hunger, and so eating is part of our intention in acting. We study in order to learn, and so studying is part of our intention in acting. And so on: our intentions are complexes of our ends and the chosen means to those ends.

Notice that (N5) has implications for some of our earlier examples. For instance, in the case of Spy, Spy dies as the chosen means to her end of avoiding revealing military secrets. Her death is *how* she will avoid revealing military secrets under torture. Hence, (N5), in conjunction with (S), implies that Spy's death amounts to suicide. However, notice a crucial difference that, in some philosophers' eyes, distinguishes Spy from Foxhole Jumper: Spy's death is her means to her end so death is part of her intention. Foxhole Jumper's death is not his chosen means to his end. His end or aim is to save his comrades *by* jumping on the grenade. His death is therefore not part of his intention. It is instead a foreseen effect of his chosen (and hence, intended) means. Thus, according to (N5), Foxhole Jumper's death is not intentional, and if (S) is correct, then Foxhole Jumper is not an instance of suicide.

I contend, however, that Foxhole Jumper should be classified as a suicide. But how can this be? Given my preferred definition (S), Foxhole Jumper would only be an instance of suicide if (N5) is incorrect. That is, Foxhole Jumper would have to be an instance of intentional self-killing, despite his death being neither the end (or aim) of his act of jumping on the grenade nor his chosen means of achieving his end of saving his fellow soldiers. But since I accept (N4) as an account of what makes death a person's intention, the only avenue for rejecting (N5) is if the other premise supporting (N5), namely (N1), should be rejected.

"Intentionally" without "intention"

I believe (N1) should be rejected.

> (N1) An individual's self-killing is intentional just in case death is the intention of the act that resulted in the individual's death.

The reasons for rejecting (N1) can be seen by returning to Foxhole Jumper. I have granted that Foxhole Jumper does not intend his death, either as an end or as a means. But I maintain that his death was intentional and hence suicide. First, note that as in Robber, Foxhole Jumper dies as a result of *self*-killing, even though there is a sense in which his death is not self-caused. After all, the grenade that kills him is thrown by an enemy solider in an attempt to kill him or his cohort, and it would be natural to see Foxhole Jumper as a war casualty—as homicide. But this overlooks our earlier observation that the "self" in (S) cannot be identified with the *cause* of one's death. Robber engages in intentional self-killing and is therefore an instance of suicide, even though the police firing their weapons at him is the cause of Robber's death. In this respect, Robber is not the cause of his own death in the manner that Despondent, Shooter, Spy, and Dissident are the causes of their own deaths. Thus, even though it is reasonable to claim that the grenade is the cause of Foxhole Jumper's death, this does not preclude his action being a self-killing nevertheless.

But in what respect is Foxhole Jumper's death intentional, given that death is not his intention? Part of the difficulty here is that English is plagued by the fact that the relationship between a person's *intention* and whether an act or outcome is *intentional* is murky. It is natural to suppose that "intentional" is the adjectival form of "intention," and since a person's intention is what she aims to bring about, either as an end or the means she has reason to pursue because it is apparently effective in realizing her end, then intentional acts or outcomes can only be those that a person intends or that form her intention. But the semantic similarity between "intention" and "intentional" can be taken too far, and in this case, restricting "intentional" only to a person's intentions, whether ends or means, is wrongheaded. Compare the relationship between "pasture" and "pastoral": the former is the origin of the latter, and while "pastoral" *can* mean "relating to pastures or the animals that graze therein," "pastoral" has other meanings. Beethoven subtitled his Sixth Symphony "the Pastoral," but its pastoral qualities have little to do with animals grazing in pastures. I propose that "intentional" likewise has a broader meaning than merely that which is part of a person's intention, and that under this broader meaning acts like Foxhole Jumper's are acts of suicide. Everything a person intends, or that is part of her intention, whether her end or means, is thereby intentional. But not everything intentional is thereby a component of a person's intention.

In what respect could "intentional" have a broader meaning? Doubtless many acts of suicide are such that death is part of the individual's intentions, either as means or as ends. In cases like Spy or Despondent, the individuals are *trying to die.* This is not so in the case of Foxhole Jumper, since death is a foreseen side effect of his chosen means, i.e., jumping on the grenade. But notice that dying still has Foxhole Jumper's *rational endorsement.* He knows that dying is the near certain result of his jumping on the grenade, and absorbing the grenade blast is his means to saving his comrades. And in that split second in which Foxhole Jumper jumps on the grenade, the foreseeability of his death almost certainly informs his deliberation, even if that deliberation takes place so rapidly as to nearly escape his notice. And unless he is also gravely depressed, for instance, his death counts in his mind as a reason *against* jumping on the grenade. He jumped on the grenade despite this danger. In essence, Foxhole Jumper endorses his own death—neither as a means nor as an end, but as a foreseeable result of the act he chooses as a means: a death that has his rational approval. In saying that Foxhole Jumper rationally endorses or approves of his own death, I am not suggesting that he *prefers* to die. Indeed, he may well hope the grenade is a dud or that he survives the blast. So too for some of our other earlier examples: Despondent might well prefer to achieve his end of relieving his anguish through some other means than death. But in both of these cases, death nevertheless has the deliberative endorsement of the individual in the circumstances in which the individual makes his/her choice. What varies is simply how death is endorsed: in Despondent's case, as a means to his end, but in Foxhole Jumper's case, as a foreseeable effect of his chosen means. It strains credulity to deny that the prospect of death does, and ought to, play a role in Despondent's and Foxhole Jumper's deliberation about their choices. And it is this fact that renders their deaths intentional: their choices amount, in effect, to a rational choice to die.

In my view, then, intentional outcomes are those that have an individual's rational endorsement in the circumstances of her action:

> (N6) A person's self-killing is intentional just in case her death has her rational endorsement in the circumstances in which she acts so as to bring about her death.

Notice that (N6) in effect encompasses (N1) without restricting "intentional" to an individual's intentions or what she narrowly intends. An individual's intentions (i.e., her ends and the chosen means to achieve those ends) have her rational endorsement. But so too can other "unintended" outcomes have a person's rational endorsement and hence be intentional.

A defense of "intentional" as rational endorsement

Why should we accept my broader account of "intentional"? First, my account makes sense of certain ways we talk about suicide. We sometimes call certain acts "suicidal" in which a person does not intend to die. Imagine describing Foxhole Jumper's actions to a young military recruit and then asking the recruit if he would be prepared to do likewise. If the recruit were to answer, "No way—that's suicidal!", the recruit does not seem to be misspeaking in calling Foxhole Jumper suicidal, despite his death not being part of his intention. This indicates that acts are often thought of as suicidal even when they are intentional in my proposed broader sense.

Second, "intentional" is closely connected with praise and blame: we praise or blame those acts or outcomes that are intentional. But notice that such praise or blame would make no sense if "intentional" were restricted merely to a person's intentions in the narrow sense suggested by (N5). For instance, Foxhole Jumper acts courageously, because death is typically an unwelcome result, and he is seeking a morally admirable end (saving his comrades) for which he knowingly endorses death, not as a means to that end, but as a foreseeable result of his chosen means. It is incoherent to even call his act courageous unless he rationally endorses his death, and in calling it courageous we implicitly concede that his self-killing is intentional. It is a suicide, albeit a morally admirable one.

Third, understanding "intentional" as I do allows that a distinction between intended and foreseen outcomes of an act such as suicide can be morally relevant even if it does not define the act. A number of philosophers defend what is known as *the doctrine of double effect*. This doctrine is widely invoked in debates about the ethics of war and abortion, and it sometimes plays a role in discussions of suicide and euthanasia as well. Double effect is a complex doctrine, but for our purposes the core idea behind it is that there is a conceptual (and sometimes moral) distinction between an outcome that a person intends to achieve through her actions and outcomes that she foresees but does not intend. In some cases, such a distinction is perfectly credible. If I enter a classroom with twenty students, I may foresee that my action will result in an odd number of people in the classroom, but there being an odd number of people is no part of my intention in entering the classroom. Indeed, I couldn't care less whether the number of people in the classroom is odd or even. My intention in walking through the door is to begin my class meeting promptly, among other things.

In my view, the distinction between intended and foreseen outcomes is not relevant to defining suicide, because according to (N6), suicide can occur, even though death is not the individual's intention, when a person kills herself intentionally by rationally endorsing her foreseen death. However, this does not mean that the distinction between intended and foreseen outcomes is not relevant to the moral *evaluation* of suicide, and my suspicion is that those seeking to show that examples such as Foxhole Jumper are not examples of suicide are seeking to exonerate such suicidal behavior by conceptual means. In other words, they believe that when self-killings have morally admirable motives, those self-killings should not be classified as suicides. Claiming that only when death is part of an individual's intention is the death intentional does turn examples such as Foxhole Jumper into something other than suicide. But this move succumbs to the worries I identified earlier about definitions of suicide being descriptive rather than value-laden. To vindicate self-killings done from morally admirable motives is itself morally admirable, but to define these away so that they are not acts of suicide is the wrong approach.

As discussed above, the English language has a word for immoral killings of others—"murder"—and a more general word for any killing of another person—"homicide." However, when it comes to self-killings we have only one general word, "suicide," to cover all self-killings, regardless of whether those killings are admirable, immoral, etc. And since the word "suicide" has acquired a strongly negative connotation, this gives rise to an understandable desire to classify admirable self-killings as something other than suicide. I would propose instead that we must treat "suicide" as a neutral concept and be willing to entertain the notion that some suicides are unjustified, imprudent, immoral, and so on, while others are not. (Maybe someday our language will develop the equivalent to "murder" with respect to self-killing—a word for unjustified or wrongful *self*-killing.) An unwillingness to do so prevents us from being as perspicuous as we can about the nature of suicide. But my understanding of intentional self-killing makes (S) evaluatively neutral while not ruling out the possibility that the distinction between intended and foreseen outcomes can matter from a moral point of view.

Fourth, understanding "intentional" as I do is necessary in order for us to treat similar cases of killing alike. Shelly Kagan[1] offers a variation on our Foxhole Jumper example. Suppose that instead of the soldier jumping on the grenade, a cowardly private pushes him onto the grenade and kills him. Note that just as in the original Foxhole Jumper example, the cowardly private does not have Foxhole Jumper's death as his *intention*. His aim is to save himself and other soldiers with the chosen means of pushing Foxhole Jumper onto the grenade, an act that the cowardly private foresees will cause Foxhole Jumper's death. Despite the soldier's death not being his intention, it seems undeniable that the cowardly private intentionally killed Foxhole Jumper by pushing him onto the grenade. But then why should we be reluctant to say, in the original Foxhole Jumper example, that Foxhole Jumper engaged in *intentional* self-killing? After all, Foxhole Jumper's death was not part of his intention either. Which person is responsible for bringing about an outcome, such as a person's death, should not make a difference to whether that outcome is intentionally brought about. If so, then we must conclude that both Foxhole Jumper and his being pushed onto the grenade are examples of intentional killings, a fact that my (N6) explains well. If Foxhole Jumper jumps on the grenade, then his foreseen death has his rational endorsement, and if the cowardly private

---

1   *The Limits of Morality* (New York: Oxford University Press, 1989), pp. 144-46.

pushes Foxhole Jumper onto the grenade, then his foreseen death has the cowardly private's endorsement. The former is intentional self-killing, the latter intentional killing.

Before considering one final reason to understand intentional self-killing as I have proposed it, let us consider how (S), understood in light of (N6), evaluates our original set of examples. Suicide is intentional self-killing, where intentional self-killings are those wherein the individual rationally endorses her own death as the chosen means or a foreseeable effect of pursuing her ends. According to this definition, Despondent, Spy, Robber, Foxhole Jumper, and Cancer Patient represent instances of suicide, whereas Skydiver and Shooter do not.

Ambivalence toward death

At this point, someone may raise a practical objection to (S) as I have described and defended it. When exactly does a person act so as to "rationally endorse" her own death? Rational endorsement is not something easy to discern from the outside, so to speak. Furthermore, as the suicide researcher Edwin Shneidman has pointed out, *ambivalence* is common among those who engage in self-destructive behavior, and actual cases of self-killing or self-harming are often quite intricate.[1] I have said little to this point about examples like Cutter. Don't such examples, where the individual is ambivalent about the prospect of death, show that whatever the theoretical merits of (S), it is of little practical use given how many suicidal individuals exhibit the ambivalence Shneidman observes?

Certainly, understanding the psychological dynamics of actual suicidal conduct, including what reasons or beliefs motivate such conduct, is not a simple matter. In particularly complex cases, mental-health professionals are sometimes called in after a person dies under ambiguous circumstances to perform what is known as a "psychiatric autopsy." Such a procedure involves examining not only a corpse, but also evidence such as the manner of death, the individual's behavior in the days leading to her death, and her mental-health history, in order to determine how the person's death is to be classified. (In the United States, all deaths are put into one of five categories: natural, accidental, homicide, suicide, or undetermined.)

---

1   *The Suicidal Mind* (Oxford: Oxford University Press, 1996), p. 133.

As I noted above, it can be difficult to pinpoint whether death has the individual's rational endorsement. Suppose, for instance, that in our Cutter example the individual in question is not rescued and ends up dying. Should her death be categorized as suicide? On its face, it appears correct to call this a self-killing. Furthermore, she most likely satisfies the condition that she believes her death is likely if she cuts herself. However, because the individual in Cutter is issuing what psychiatrists term a "cry for help," in which she hopes to draw attention to her plight with behavior that merely mimics the behavior of those who are fully suicidal, it is not obviously an *intentional* self-killing. In terms of my earlier language, dying does not have Cutter's (full) deliberative endorsement. Yet at the same time, calling her death accidental is awkward, too: she seems to recognize that her behavior *could* end up killing her, and she does it anyway. Cutter's death thus belongs in an odd category: an unintentional but also non-accidental self-inflicted death. (Much the same could perhaps be said about Shooter.)

Or consider this example:

> **Addict**: A man with a longstanding heroin addiction prepares to inject himself with an unprecedented amount of his favored drug. He recognizes that this dosage could be fatal, but his craving for a high is overwhelming. Though he doesn't inject himself with the potentially lethal dose in order to kill himself, he is also profoundly ashamed about the wretched condition that his addiction has created. He injects the heroin expecting that he may not wake up from the catatonic state the drug produces.

Like Cutter, Addict is ambivalent about his own self-harming behavior. While it cannot be said that he intentionally seeks his own death, it also cannot be said that his death is accidental, given his awareness that his actions may well kill him. He appears to accept or foresee death, though his death is not obviously intentional. Is his conduct suicidal?

These are examples where the individuals are ambivalent about whether they wish to die. In other cases, the nature of the method chosen appears to rule out ambivalence. A person who throws herself in front of a train *could* be issuing a cry for help, but given that her means of doing so is so lethal (especially in comparison to other ways of issuing a cry for help, such as taking pills), it becomes hard to imagine that her death is at all ambivalent. Therefore, the only reasonable conclusion in such a case is that the self-killing was intentional and therefore suicide. Such examples highlight that the relationship between the action a person takes in pursuit of a goal, the goal itself, and her intentions are complex. Sometimes the sort of action a person takes in pursuit of a goal is strong evidence of how seriously she is seeking the goal, and in the case of suicide, strong evidence of the degree to which the person's dying is intentional. Generally speaking, the more lethal the method with which a person chooses to die, the more probable it is that a person's death is intentional and thus the more probable it is that her self-killing should be considered a suicide.

There are, I believe, two broad responses to this phenomenon of suicidal ambivalence. One is to suggest that it makes more sense not to think of individuals' behavior as suicidal or not but as a matter of degree. In other words, we should think of various self-killings or acts of self-harm not as either suicidal or not suicidal, but as more or less suicidal. The psychiatrist Aaron Beck has developed a well-known questionnaire that assesses how suicidal a person's behavior or attitudes are on a numerical scale.[1] This questionnaire, which has proven to be very effective as a tool for predicting suicide, asks various questions about the person's mood, previous suicidal behavior, and other factors, and assigns a numerical value to the person's overall suicidal intent. Thus, Beck's questionnaire views suicidal behavior less as an either/or matter but as resting at different points along a continuum. Treating suicidal behavior in this way is certainly more faithful to the psychological reality of a wide spectrum of suicidal behavior. In addition, such an approach fits well with my account of suicide as rationally endorsed or intentional self-killing. Though Beck does not put the matter this way, perhaps suicide comes in degrees precisely because the rational endorsement of one's death comes in degrees.

Yet saying that an individual's death was *mostly* suicidal or that one person's death was *more* the product of suicide than another person's death may seem psychologically and practically unsatisfying. A parent seeking emotional closure concerning the death of a child may feel that such descriptions leave painful and unresolved ambiguities. Similarly, such an approach to classifying suicidal behavior would likely prove burdensome in the legal realm, where judgments can sometimes hinge on whether a person died as a result of suicide.

---

1   Aaron T. Beck, Maria Kovacs, and Arlene Weissman, "Assessment of suicidal intention: The Scale for Suicidal Ideation," *Journal of Consulting and Clinical Psychology* 47 (1979): 343-52.

A second approach is to argue that we need a wider set of categories in order to provide an adequate framework for classifying self-harm. As we have observed, our language does not provide us with a rich vocabulary for thinking about self-harm and self-killing. German has at least three different terms to speak of self-killing, and ancient Greek had at least a dozen, including terms translatable as "to seize death," "to leave the light," "to go voluntarily to the underworld," "to kill oneself," and "to dispose of oneself." This may not seem like a terribly important fact, but language can influence thought and practice, and, in particular, it can place artificial constraints on how actions and practices are described. In the case of self-harm and self-killing, perhaps our thinking has been shaped, even limited, by the small vocabulary we have to address these phenomena.

Hence, the variety of self-harms or self-killings might be better captured if we broadened the language surrounding them. I have argued elsewhere that many self-killings can be compared to the legal category of manslaughter.[1] Manslaughter (at least the involuntary variety) occurs when one person kills another through her own recklessness even though she did not intend to harm or kill another. For instance, someone who gets behind the wheel of his car while drunk and ends up striking and killing a pedestrian can be charged with manslaughter. I propose that at least some self-killings are like manslaughter in that they result from a person's recklessly subjecting herself to harm even without fully intending harm or death. So in our Cutter example, the individual who cuts herself in this way is knowingly putting herself at risk of harm or death much in the same fashion that a drunk driver is knowingly putting others at risk. Thus, we could say that Cutter is an example of *self-manslaughter*, rather than suicide or innocent accidental death.

In the end, though, suicidal ambivalence poses an important practical challenge to my proposed definition of suicide. Moreover, I see this not as a drawback of (S) but as a strength: recall that I earlier suggested that an adequate definition of suicide should be value-neutral and make sense of clear cut cases on either side of the divide. Moreover, an adequate definition should also help resolve controversial examples. I contend that I have done so with Foxhole Jumper, by showing how under my expanded understanding of "intentional," his death was an intentional self-killing. Yet ultimately, an adequate definition, where it cannot resolve controversial or difficult examples,

---

1   "Self-manslaughter and the forensic classification of self-inflicted deaths," *Journal of Medical Ethics* 33 (2007): 155-57.

should at least help us understand *why* these are controversial or difficult examples. In other words, an adequate definition of suicide should tell us why hard cases are *hard*. (S) does that with respect to suicidal ambivalence: many self-destructive or self-harming acts do not seem to be readily classifiable as suicides or not. But according to (S), this reflects the further fact that many such acts are performed by agents who are ambivalent about suicide, that is, agents for whom suicide is only to some extent, rather than wholeheartedly, rationally endorsed.

Can Suicide Be Coerced?

The one example we have not discussed yet is Dissident:

> **Dissident**: A political dissident is sentenced to die for criticizing a to-talitarian government. However, his sentence is that he must administer a lethal injection to himself or the state will forcibly kill him. The dissident chooses the former option and dies by injecting himself with a cocktail of fatal drugs.

Some take examples such as Dissident not to be examples of suicide at all. Why might we deny that Dissident ends his life through suicide? Dissident's death does result from self-killing (he administers the lethal injection), but his choice to self-kill is the result of *coercion* on the part of government authorities. Hence, his self-killing does not involve an intention to die, and so, according to our proposed definition (S), Dissident's behavior is not suicidal.

To determine whether this conclusion is correct, we need to put the notion of *coercion* under our philosophical microscope. Typically, a person X is coerced when another person Y interferes with her conduct so as to give X powerful reasons to do Y's bidding. So for instance, if Y robs X at knifepoint, X gives Y her purse because Y has threatened to stab her if she does not. X does choose to give up her purse, but only because Y has given her a powerful reason to do so, and in giving up the purse, X ends up giving Y what Y desired in the first place. Similarly, in Dissident, the dissident only chooses to end his own life because the state has promised to end it for him if he won't. Thus, given the option between self-killing and being the victim of homicide, the dissident is coerced into choosing the former.

However, I believe that examples like Dissident should be classified as suicides. Indeed, there is nothing contradictory about a self-killing being coerced and its being an act of intentional self-killing. The end for which the dissident engages in self-killing is to avoid an outcome (his being killed by the authorities) that he judges to be worse than his self-killing, yet his self-killing is nevertheless intentional. He aims to die by giving himself the injection, which he recognizes will kill him. That his ends or reasons originate in the state's coercion do not seem to change the fact that he dies as a consequence of intentional self-killing.

Furthermore, I suspect that this proposal is motivated by the same understandable but ill-advised desire we noted above: to redefine "suicide" so that admirable self-killings turn out not to be suicides. Dissident (and Spy) are similar to self-killings such as those of Socrates and of religious martyrs, self-killings that many would not want to criticize or condemn. Not to belabor the point: instead of defining away admirable self-killings as something other than "suicide," we should strive for a value-neutral definition of suicide that allows us to talk of justified, morally permissible, suicides.

One final case may cause difficulty for my conclusion that coerced self-killing can nevertheless be suicide.

> **Hypnotized**: A hypnotist manages to put his rival into a hypnotic trance and directs his rival to put a gun to his head and pull the trigger. The rival dies due to the gunshot.

Hypnotized does not seem like an example of suicide, even though it appears to be an intentional self-killing. The rival instigates a course of action that results in his death, so this is a self-killing. And insofar as the hypnotist leads the rival to kill himself, the self-killing appears to be coerced. So is this a coerced suicide, contrary to first appearances?

I am skeptical that the rival's death is coerced. Recall that as we characterized coercion, a person X is coerced when another person Y interferes with her conduct so as to give X powerful *reasons* to do Y's bidding. While I am not an expert on hypnotic states, it is not obvious that in cases like Hypnotized a person is responding to reasons provided by the hypnotist. Hypnotism operates on the basis of "hypnotic suggestion," but such suggestion does not provide the hypnotized individual with reasons to do what the hypnotist suggests. The hypnotized rival is merely directed, by means of verbal suggestion, to put the gun to his head. Hypnosis thus seems to operate by working *around* an individual's reasoning capacities, rather than engaging with those capacities. In this respect, the rival's suicide is a kind of non-rational or automatic action. He is not coerced into suicide, but compelled into self-killing, his conduct controlled by the hypnotist much in the way a puppeteer guides a marionette. In contrast, the state provides Dissident with a reason to take her own life, a reason on which she acts, and the state thus coerces her into suicide.

Thus, Hypnotized does not represent a counterexample to my claim that coerced self-killings can be suicides because the rival is not coerced into self-killing. But the example might remain troubling if, according to my definition (S), the rival engages in suicide. Yet the same considerations that show that the rival's death was not coerced also show why the rival's self-killing was not intentional. Note that in my view, to say a suicide is an intentional self-killing is to say that the self-killing has the individual's rational or deliberative endorsement. Again, the rival does not seem to act on any discernible reasons in ending his life. He is the victim of the hypnotist's automatic suggestion, and in this regard he does not choose to die at all. The rival's self-killing is not intentional, and, if anything, the hypnotist murders him.

Conclusion

I have tried to argue here that, if we strive to define suicide in a purely descriptive way that captures the clear cut cases, resolves some controversial cases, and provides an account of why hard cases are hard, then to define suicide as intentional self-killing is adequate, and many of the objections to this definition rest on a shaky understanding of what makes an outcome intentional. That being said, it should be noted that whatever the merits of this definition, its application in actual practice—i.e., using the definition to identify *actual* self-killings and acts of self-harm—is a different and probably thornier matter.

Further Reading

Donnelly's 1998 anthology contains many of the seminal articles on the nature of suicide. Suzanne Stern-Gillett (1987) significantly influenced my own thinking about the nature of suicide. Other insightful discussions of the nature of suicide and the difficulties in defining it include Kupfer (1990), Beauchamp

(1992); chapter 5 of Fairbairn (1995); and chapter 8 of Luper (2009). McIntyre (2009) provides an overview of the distinction between intentional and fore-seen outcomes. Chapter 6 of Glover (1990) criticizes this doctrine. I defend the notion that some self-inflicted deaths are analogous to manslaughter in Cholbi (2007). Aaron Beck's Suicidal Ideation Scale (1979) can be acquired at http://www.beckscales.com.

two

The Moral Impermissibility of Suicide

If suicide is allowed then everything is allowed. If anything is not allowed then suicide is not allowed. This throws a light on the nature of ethics, for suicide is, so to speak, the elementary sin.[1]

A GREAT DEAL OF Western philosophical thinking about suicide has concerned itself with the question of whether it is ever morally permissible for individuals to commit suicide. In this chapter we will consider the main arguments that have been given for the conclusion that it is *never* the case that it is morally permissible for individuals to commit suicide. Because Christianity in particular has exerted so much influence on our thinking about suicide, we will first consider three arguments for the moral impermissibility of suicide

---

1   Ludwig Wittgenstein, *Notebooks: 1914-1916*, trans G.H. von Wright and G.E.M. Anscombe (Chicago: University of Chicago Press, 1979), p. 91.

that are closely associated with the Christian tradition, before turning to several non-religious arguments for its impermissibility.

Christian Arguments for the Impermissibility of Suicide

The arrival of Christianity is the most important event in Western philosophical thinking about suicide. Prior to the Christian era, the ancient philosophers of the Mediterranean world held a diversity of views about the ethics of suicide. Most of the ancient political and legal authorities took a dim view of it, but philosophers such as Plato, Aristotle, and the Stoics did not share a common view on the ethics of suicide. Plato, for instance, defended the gloomy view that suicide is impermissible because it amounts to releasing our souls from the bodies the gods have placed us in as a form of punishment. Despite this, Plato was willing to forgive suicide if the individual in question had a morally corrupted soul or was acting from a sense of shame at having committed a grossly unjust act. And, unsurprisingly, Plato was also willing to forgive those who took their lives by judicial order, as his teacher Socrates did. Plato's student Aristotle said even less about suicide but seemed attracted to the thought that it was sometimes wrong because only the political leaders of a community have the right to decide that a person may die. Later ancient thinkers often thought of suicide as the prudent option if the goods that make for a valuable life are not forthcoming. The Stoic writers Cicero and Seneca, for example, argued that we require various "natural advantages" in order to live happy and virtuous lives. A person in poor physical health may find living virtuously or happily quite difficult, making it rational and honorable for such a person to end her life. As Cicero put it, "When a man's circumstances contain a preponderance of things in accordance with nature, it is appropriate for him to remain alive; when he possesses or sees in prospect a majority of the contrary things, it is appropriate for him to depart from life."[1]

On the whole, ancient Greek and Roman philosophers approached the ethics of suicide as a secular question of personal virtue, well-being, or one's relationship to the larger community. The dawn of Christianity fundamentally altered how Western thinkers approached the ethics of suicide. From

---

1   Cicero, *De Finibus Bonorum et Malorum*, trans. H. Rackham (London: William Heinemann, 1914), section III.

the earliest days of the Christian era, Christian leaders and intellectuals were suspicious of suicide. Their suspicions generated many of the classical religious arguments for the moral impermissibility of suicide. A number of historians have noted that the leaders of the early Christian Church worried that by describing the afterlife in heaven in such inviting terms, while emphasizing that our earthly existence is a litany of hardships and suffering, they were inadvertently encouraging suicide among Christians. One Christian sect in particular, the Donatists, encouraged suicide as an act of martyrdom. Add to this that the biblical texts addressing suicide are few in number and do not roundly condemn the practice (the suicide of Judas, Jesus' betrayer, is depicted as the honorable fulfillment of divine prophecy, for example), and it becomes understandable why Christian thinkers saw a need to provide a rationale for their ethical opposition to suicide. They found such rationales by reconceptualizing the ethical significance of suicide, directing attention from questions of one's well-being or one's relationship to other human beings and toward the significance of suicide for an individual's relationship to God. As the historian Georges Minois puts it, Christians have usually understood suicide as "an affair between the devil and the individual sinner,"[1] and until the past several centuries, Christian practices reflected the belief that suicide was a sin. Many of those who died by suicide were denied Christian burial, a prerequisite for entry into heaven, and in some cases their corpses were defiled.

But here our purposes are not historical, but philosophical: so are the religiously based arguments for the moral impermissibility of suicide sound?

The natural law argument

Let us begin with St. Thomas Aquinas, the most influential of all Catholic philosophers, for a statement of one of these arguments. In his massive work *Summa Theologica*, Aquinas offers the canonical expression of the natural law argument for the moral impermissibility of suicide:

> Because everything naturally loves itself, the result being that everything naturally keeps itself in being, and resists corruption so far as it can. Wherefore suicide is contrary to the inclination of nature and to charity,

---

1   G. Minois, *History of Suicide: Voluntary Death in Western Culture* (Baltimore: Johns Hopkins Press, 1999), p. 300.

whereby every man should love himself. Hence suicide is always a mortal sin, as being contrary to the natural law and to charity.[1]

The most obscure aspect of the natural law argument is Aquinas's premise that suicide is contrary to nature or to "natural law." After all, many human practices seem "unnatural"—cosmetic surgery, the use of artificial organs or limbs, entering a virtual reality machine—but few people think these practices are morally impermissible. So what could it mean to say that suicide is contrary to nature or to natural law, and why should we be convinced that an action's being contrary to nature or to natural law makes it morally impermissible?

Though it sounds a bit archaic to hear people discuss ethical issues in terms of "natural law" nowadays, it is not completely unheard of (for instance, some oppose homosexuality or same-sex relationships on the basis that these are contrary to natural law). But historically, the thought that suicide is somehow "unnatural" has been very influential. Before considering whether the natural law argument succeeds in showing that suicide is impermissible because it is at odds with natural law, it is important to appreciate what Aquinas is *not* saying. To say that an act is contrary to natural law is not to say that it is contrary to the *scientific laws of nature*, for example, Newton's three laws of motion. After all, no act could be contrary to a law of nature, since if a law of nature really is a law, it holds true no matter what human beings think or do. Human beings cannot act contrary to the law of gravity.

Aquinas's natural laws are instead better thought of as the basic principles that guide an organism so that it can survive and flourish. Implicit in his argument is the claim that every living being naturally strives to preserve itself and to keep itself free from disease, injury, or "corruption." In the case of human beings, God implanted in us the desire or "inclination" to love ourselves and seek our own preservation. Chief among these is the desire to live, which in turn gives rise to many more specific desires, such as the desires to eat, drink, and so on. More importantly, God gave us the inclination to seek our own happiness. Note that unlike the physical laws of nature, these natural laws can be violated. It is possible to do things that are harmful to ourselves or that make us unhappy. Aquinas believed, nevertheless, that by using reason, we can figure out what sorts of choices lead to happiness and continued life. Suicide, according to the natural law argument, is therefore wrong because

---

1   *Summa Theologica*, trans. Fathers of the English Dominican Province (New York: Cosimo, 2007), part II, Q64, A5.

it is unnatural. For a person to end her own life is contrary to her nature, a nature fashioned by God.

Suicide is clearly contrary to Aquinas's natural laws. In taking our own lives, Aquinas says, we are acting against our own nature. But is this a good argument for the moral impermissibility of suicide? Before considering this question, a caution: it is tempting to dismiss religious arguments for the impermissibility of suicide because they rest on controversial religious premises. After all, Aquinas's natural law argument assumes a great deal of religious dogma—that God exists, that God created human beings with a natural inclination to survive, and so on. These are obviously highly debatable premises, and philosophers, theologians, and others have spent centuries debating them. However, I propose that since our particular interest here is in the ethics of suicide, we should put aside worries about the truth of these religious premises and simply grant them for the sake of argument. (As we shall see, there are plenty of challenges to the religious arguments that do not take issue with their religious premises.)

One objection to the natural law argument that can be easily answered is that suicide cannot be "unnatural" since many people do it. Again, however, Aquinas's claim is not that suicide violates the laws of nature, nor even that suicide is unnatural because it is rare. His claim is that suicide is contrary to what makes us human animals and contrary to the pursuit of happiness, which culminates in realizing our human nature. In the worldview of medieval Christian philosophers, human beings are happy when they fully act in accordance with the kinds of beings they are. Since human beings are living, happiness-seeking creatures, and since suicide makes both of these goals impossible, suicide can be said to be unnatural.

There are, however, two principal criticisms of the natural law argument. The first is that it is not so obvious that we have such a strong inclination to preserve ourselves or to protect our bodies from harm or injury. To put it bluntly, human beings are often an aggressive, violent, self-destructive species, prone to war, excessive risk taking, and substance abuse. The evidence from human behavior might suggest that if God created human beings with an inclination to preserve ourselves, that inclination competes with other inclinations that tend to cause us harm. Psychoanalysts such as Freud went so far as to posit a primal "death drive," i.e., a motivation that leads us toward self-destruction.[1] Defenders of the natural law argument have a ready reply to

---

1   See, for example, Freud's *Beyond the Pleasure Principle*, trans. James Strachey (New York: Liveright, 1961).

this objection, however: when people behave in self-destructive ways, they are behaving irrationally. The person who smokes knowing it causes cancer; the leader who leads his country into a futile war; and the driver who recklessly cruises the highway—all of these individuals either fail to recognize that their behavior may harm or kill themselves, or they recognize this but are unable to control their desires to behave in these ways. God gave us the power of reason to help us discern what is good for us and what conforms to our nature, and reason teaches us that we ought to take care to preserve our lives. It is no strike against the claim that suicide is unnatural, defenders of the natural law argument might say, that some people use their reason improperly and thereby end up acting in ways that are unnatural.

Here, however, a more serious objection looms. Suppose that God did grant us the inclination to preserve our lives, and that since self-preservation is generally good for us, we benefit from having such an inclination. The natural law argument thus answers what seems like an intricate question—whether it is rational for a person to end her life—with a simple response: it is always irrational to end one's life because this is contrary to a God-given inclination that is *generally* good or beneficial to us. Does it follow, though, that we act irrationally if we act in opposition to this inclination of self-preservation, as the natural law argument claims? The argument appears to rest on the thesis that it is *necessarily* irrational to destroy oneself. What makes an act rational is a highly contentious philosophical question, but many suicidal people clearly do not think that ending their lives would be an irrational act. They may believe, as the Stoics did, that when the future is sufficiently bleak and unhappy, a rational person should consider suicide and that it is only an irrational fear of death that prevents people from seriously considering whether they have good reasons to end their lives. To show "charity" toward oneself may justify ending one's life, just as showing charity to a wounded animal may justify ending its life. If the purpose or aim of the inclination of self-preservation that God provided us is to benefit us and make us happy, it seems positively irrational to continue one's life when doing so does not benefit us or makes us miserable. In those cases, it would appear irrational to follow this inclination of self-preservation. These worries illustrate a fundamental tension in the natural law outlook: by acting rationally we will become happy *and* we will find it irrational to end our lives. But that is exactly what some suicidal people appear to conclude: it is rational to end their lives because those lives are, or are likely to be, very *unhappy*. Again, such conclusions may be wrong, but the natural law argument for the impermissibility of suicide appears to simply avoid that issue.

The property argument

A second common religious argument appeals to the premise that human beings in effect steal from God by engaging in suicide. According to this property argument, human beings, having been created by God, are God's property, and just as with any other piece of property, it is a wrong to the property owner if others destroy that property. Hence, while God may permissibly destroy his human creations, human beings may not. Suicide (and murder) are therefore impermissible.

The property argument draws upon some intuitively compelling commonplaces about property. When a person rightfully owns something, other people are not morally permitted to interfere with that thing, much less destroy it. Moreover, assuming God created us, this seems to make us his property, in the same way that an artist creating a painting or sculpture gives the artist property rights in that artwork. Thus, if human beings are God's property, the property argument would appear to be a sound argument for the moral impermissibility of suicide.

Yet there are challenges facing the property argument, stemming both from the claim that God owns us in the way that we own property and from the claim that it is wrong to destroy God's property through suicide. One challenge is that human beings seem like a strange kind of property, if they are property at all. Can human beings even be owned? Recall that the institution of slavery was an institution predicated on human beings' owning one another. But opponents of slavery have consistently argued that human beings are not the sorts of things that can be owned. Similarly, children were once thought of in many cultures as the property of their parents, yet many of us now think that even though parents have many rights with respect to their children, they do not have property rights in their children. Indeed, if parents did own their children, then parents would presumably have the right to treat their children the way they treat other forms of property. To take this claim to its logical conclusion, if children were property, parents could sell them, discard them in the trash, or kill them and eat them. But the gross immorality of such behavior is a good indication that we should not think of children as property in the first place. So if neither children nor slaves are property, what reason is there to suppose that human beings in general are property, even God's property? Land, sandwiches, stock in corporations, a camera, a plane ticket: these are the sorts of things that definitely *can* be owned and so function as property, but they seem different from human beings in important ways that have suggested to many that human beings are not ownable. It may be hard to say exactly what differentiates human beings from things that can be owned. Perhaps it is our capacity to reason, our ability to experience pleasure and pain, or our (alleged) free will. But we need not take a stand on what feature of human beings might distinguish us from things that can be owned as property in order to have moral reservations about the claim that we are God's property.

A second challenge to the property argument is that it is far from clear how killing oneself is a harm or a wrong to God in the way that taking other people's property is a harm or a wrong to them. Why is theft wrong, at least in the usual cases? Because human beings use property to meet their needs and satisfy their wants. When someone steals another person's food or money, the person whose property is stolen will find it harder to meet their needs or satisfy their 'wants. Hence, theft harms those whose property is stolen. This wouldn't be true if the goods we treat as property were not scarce. If, for instance, food was infinitely abundant, then stealing other people's food would not harm them, since there would be more than enough food to go around. But how would "stealing" God's property by killing yourself harm God? Religious people disagree about the exact nature of God, of course, but many believe that God is immaterial and omnipotent. However, if God is immaterial, then it becomes mysterious what need or want of God is served by his owning us. How then would our killing ourselves destroy something of value to an immaterial God? Similarly, if God is omnipotent, then God could simply create anew any person who killed herself. Hence, for an omnipotent God, there are no scarce goods. At the very least, therefore, defenders of the property argument owe us an explanation of how God is harmed by human suicide.

A third concern with the property argument is how to square the argument with the common religious belief that God is all-loving. According to Christian teachings, God loves all human beings, even the most miserable and sinful. If God loves us, why should he not allow us to do what seems to be in our best interests, even if that turns out to be destroying his property by suicide? The property argument has struck even some religious thinkers as presenting an unflattering picture of a God more preoccupied with losing his property than by the sufferings of the creatures that God supposedly created in his image.

A final objection to the property argument is that it does not necessarily follow from the premise that human beings are God's property that it is impermissible to destroy that property via suicide. This is because sometimes the destruction of property is justified in order to prevent serious harm to oneself. If, completely without warning or provocation, my neighbor's vicious dog attacks me as I walk to my mailbox, surely I have the right to attack back in self-defense, which could result in the dog's death. If I end up killing the dog in self-defense, I have destroyed my neighbor's property, but I have done so with a powerful moral justification on my side: if I hadn't killed the dog, I would have suffered terrible harm. And it hardly seems to matter if the property in question is God's. If when suffering from frostbite I burn firewood from trees I chopped down, then if the trees are God's property, was it wrong for me to destroy that property? Surely the same reasoning applies when the property is my body, which (according to the property argument) is owned by God. If I am diagnosed with a terminal disease that will cause me to suffer a slow, lingering, debilitating death, do I *have* to put up with such a death because if I killed myself I would be destroying God's property? Probably not.

The gift argument

A final religious argument is that suicide is morally impermissible because life is a gift from God. According to the gift argument, suicide is a mark of ingratitude to God. Because God gave us life as a gift, we should be thankful to God for that gift, and suicide, rather than showing gratitude, amounts to a rejection of God's gift.

In my observation, the gift argument exerts a powerful hold on many religious people, probably because it expresses very succinctly the conviction that life is precious and that we should appreciate it. The success of the argument turns on whether the metaphor of life as a gift withstands critical scrutiny.

One challenge for the gift argument is metaphysical: who is the recipient of this gift of life? Normally, a gift is given to someone or to a group of people. Hence, the recipient of the gift must already exist, in some fashion or other, in order to be the recipient or beneficiary of the gift. But note that in the gift argument, existence *is* the gift. I was, according to this argument, given the gift of life by God. But there is no "I" to receive this gift, since I exist as the effect of the gift's being given in the first place. So how then can I be both the gift and its recipient? Admittedly, we sometimes speak of giving a child or an animal "the gift of life." Yet this metaphysical challenge—that you must exist in order to receive a gift, which is itself existence—suggests that we should not take such talk literally.

A traditional response for advocates of the gift argument to this metaphysical challenge is to invoke a dualistic conception of human nature. According to dualists, each human being has a non-material soul that can exist without the human body. In many religions, the soul (or perhaps the mind or consciousness) is the part of us that continues to exist even after the death of our bodies. If this were true, dualism would provide an answer to the challenge about who the recipient of the gift of life is: the gift's recipient is the person's soul, and the body itself is the gift. Unfortunately, though, the appeal to dualism is likely to persuade only those who share a religious outlook. A full discussion of the merits of such dualism cannot be undertaken here, but suffice it to say that many philosophers and scientists are skeptical that human beings have non-material souls that can survive the death of the body. First, dualists are hard pressed to explain certain undeniable facts about the relationship between mind and body. For instance, my mind seems intimately connected to my body inasmuch as some changes in my body produce changes in the states of my brain. These changes in my brain then appear to correlate with changes in my mental states: when I feel the sensation of thirst, this corresponds to changes in my body and changes in my brain. These observations are not incompatible with the dualistic claim that our minds are non-material souls. But surely the simpler explanation for the close relationship between the state of our bodies and mental states is that our mental states *are* the state of our bodies—more specifically, states of the brain—and do not occur in a non-material soul.

The second classic problem for dualism is how to explain the apparent causal interaction between non-material souls and the material world. Our minds are causally impacted by objects in the material world (as when our retinas are stimulated by light rays, transmitting images through our optic nerve into the brain, etc.). Objects in the material world are also causally impacted by our minds (as when choosing to get a drink results in my moving my arms and fingers). Dualism leaves us with a serious mystery as to how such interaction is possible. The interaction between mind and body appears to require that it take place *somewhere*. Yet if the mind is in fact an immaterial soul, not located in space at all, how can it change or be changed by the body, which is located in space? When our retinas are stimulated by light rays, transmitting images into our optic nerve, the visual images do not (according to the dualist) occur in the brain but in our immaterial souls. Yet how this takes place is puzzling indeed.

Of course, our discussion only scratches the surface of the debate between mind–body dualists and their opponents. Yet we should be loath to salvage the gift argument by relying on a highly controversial claim. In the end then, those who think that the metaphysical challenge to the gift argument is a potent one are likely to conclude that invoking dualism adds to the mystery rather than resolving it. A more direct response to this objection is to question the premise that in order to be the recipient of a gift, or more generally, to be benefitted, a person must already exist. It seems reasonable to think a person can be *harmed* by being brought into existence. For example, imagine that a woman has a treatable infectious disease that increases the probability that any children she conceives during the course of the disease will have a birth defect, such as a heart defect. Suppose that the woman then gives birth to Angela, and Angela has a heart defect. Many people would say that Angela was harmed by being brought into existence, since had her mother waited to conceive until after her disease had been cured, Angela would not have been born with the heart defect. Thus, Angela was harmed by being brought into existence. This conclusion is helpful in answering the metaphysical objection to the gift argument against suicide, because being benefitted and being harmed are simply opposite sides of the same coin. If a person, such as Angela, is harmed by being brought into existence, that is, she is made worse off by being brought into existence, then so too can a person be benefitted or made better off by being brought into existence. Therefore, it is possible that although a person may not yet exist, she can be benefitted by being brought into existence, and so it is intelligible to think of life as a benefit or a gift.

Nevertheless, some philosophers are unconvinced that life should be thought of as a gift or a benefit to those who do not yet exist. First, some people's lives are terrible, and it may be difficult for those people to swallow the idea that their rotten lives were any gift at all. I would not, for instance, have wanted to try to persuade the average medieval peasant living during the time of the Great Plague that her life, which was likely to be poor, short, painful, and degrading, was any gift at all. However, if God's gift of life turns out to have been an ill-chosen or almost worthless gift, then it is hard to see how much is owed to God in the way of gratitude, making it equally hard to see how disposing of this gift through suicide amounts to an act of ingratitude. Therefore, even if advocates of the gift argument can show how it is *possible* for a person's life to be a gift or a benefit to her, it doesn't follow that anyone's *actual* life is a gift or a benefit to her. That would seem to depend on how good the gift is for its recipient.

A second reason for skepticism about life being a benefit or a gift even to those who do not yet exist arises from what Derek Parfit has called the *non-identity problem*.[1] Returning to our example of Angela, suppose that instead of conceiving Angela, the mother had waited to conceive until after her disease had been cured. The child so conceived would be different from Angela in a number of ways. For one thing, the child would result from the union of different sperm and egg cells than the ones that would have produced Angela, and would therefore be genetically different from Angela in many ways (and, in turn, would differ from Angela physically, psychologically, etc.). Furthermore, the uterine environment in which this child develops would likely be different from the one in which Angela would have developed. It seems likely that the child so conceived would be sufficiently different from Angela that the child would not be Angela at all. I don't mean that the child could not be named "Angela"; I mean instead that the possible child conceived under circumstances very different from those in which Angela was conceived would not *be* Angela. But here the non-identity problem intervenes: in order for Angela to have been harmed by being brought into existence, it would have to be the case that she—Angela—was harmed (made worse off) by her mother conceiving her in the circumstances that led to Angela's heart defect rather than Angela having been conceived in circumstances where she would not have had the heart defect. However, according to the line of reasoning we just considered, the child conceived in the latter circumstances would not be Angela, from which it follows that *Angela* was not harmed by being brought into existence. Indeed, the non-identity problem appears to show that not only is no one harmed by being brought into existence, but neither is anyone benefitted in that way either, thus making it impossible for being brought into existence (by God giving you life, say) to be a gift to you.

Suppose that a woman learns that if she conceives during a certain six-month window, the child she conceives will enjoy immunity from almost

---

1   *Reasons and Persons* (Oxford: Oxford University Press, 1987), pp. 351-64.

every fatal illness, such as heart disease or cancer. If she conceives within that window, is the child born thereby—let us call him Bruce—benefitted insofar as he is immune to these fatal illnesses? Advocates of the non-identity problem would argue "no": the *actual* child Bruce is not the child the woman might have conceived (but did not) outside the six-month window, so the actual child Bruce is not made better off by having been conceived as he was. His immunity is doubtless *good* for Bruce, but *he did not benefit* from being conceived under the circumstances that conferred the immunity upon him.

The literature on the non-identity problem has grown rapidly, and I will not attempt to outline that literature. Suffice it to say, there is no philosophical consensus about whether or how the non-identity problem can be solved. This in itself is unfortunate for proponents of the gift argument, for it suggests that like an appeal to mind–body dualism, appealing to the notion that life can in fact be a gift or benefit to those who do not yet exist is at best controversial.

This is not to say that proponents of the gift argument lack possible responses to the problem. One response is to deny the claim of non-identity. The non-identity problem gets its force from the idea that changes in DNA and a fetus's uterine environment, for instance, are changes in the identity of a person, so Angela would not be Angela were she conceived from different DNA, had she developed in a different uterine environment, etc. This claim rests on a fairly strict conception of what makes for "sameness" of persons. Yet we often speak of a person being or remaining the same person despite quite substantial changes in that person. An 80-year old woman is (we suppose) the same person as her two-year-old self from 78 years ago, even though almost everything about the two individuals (their mass, volume, brain structure, mental life, intelligence, etc.) is radically different. If two such radically different individuals are nevertheless the same person, can we not suppose that two individuals are nevertheless the same person despite having different genetic makeups and having developed in different uterine environments— that Bruce and his non-existent counterpart, and Angela and her non-existent counterpart, are the same person? The non-identity problem thus rests on a weighty assumption about the identity of persons: that features such as one's genetic makeup and uterine environment are *essential* to a person, that they constitute her identity and make a person who she is. This may be the controversial assumption driving the non-identity problem.

Some advocates of the gift argument may respond to the non-identity problem by reminding us that it is life itself that God gives us, and it is life itself for which we should not be ungrateful. Consider a case more extreme than Angela's: a child, Callie, is born with a horrible defect that means she will live for only a few very painful years before dying. Callie is harmed by her existence, but not, as the non-identity problem would require, because she is made worse off by existing. Rather, her life is sufficiently bad that living as she did is worse than not living at all. If Callie's living is a harm to her, but not because she is worse than some other "Callie" that could have been conceived in different circumstances, then this appears to provide a way of making sense of life as a gift that circumvents, rather than solves, the non-identity problem. For it would appear to follow that a person's life could likewise be a benefit to her, even if she is not better off than she would have been had she been conceived in different circumstances.

But note that the conclusion here is a limited one: even if life could be a benefit, it is only a benefit to those who, unlike Callie, have lives that are worth living, i.e., lives that are better than not having lived at all. Recall my earlier observation that many lives are emphatically bad, and not worth living. If this is so, then even if some lives are gifts inasmuch as they are good enough to be better than not having lived, many lives lack this property and are not gifts at all. The gift argument might therefore show that the lives of many normal, comfortable people throughout the world are, on balance, gifts to them, gifts they should not end prematurely lest they show ingratitude to God. But the gift argument would then only show that many, not all, suicides are wrong, since life is not always a gift.

Beyond these metaphysical questions, a second general worry about the gift argument is that it is not so clear that our duty of gratitude requires us to stay alive as long as we are able. We ought to express gratitude for the gifts we receive, so if life is a gift from God, we ought to express our gratitude for that gift. However, this duty is a limited one and tends to diminish over time, and it is also possible to express insufficient gratitude. If my grandfather brought me a rare Chinese vase from his recent travels in Asia, I ought to thank him, but I am not required to express gratitude each and every time I speak to him henceforth. Likewise, it would be disrespectful to my grandfather if I used the rare Chinese vase he brought me from his archaeological dig as a spittoon. But not every use of the vase that is contrary to his preferences expresses ingratitude; for example, if he desires that I display it in a glass case, but I place it on my fireplace mantel, I am not showing ingratitude. Indeed, as we saw in our discussion of the property argument, to have a property right in something gives a person a broad right to do what she wishes with it. In the case of a gift, this confers upon its recipient a right to do largely what she pleases with it, even if this does not accord with the preferences of the gift giver. It also seems possible for this gift to outlive its usefulness. A person in an aging or diseased body could well be grateful to God for having had the opportunity to live, but if the gift of life is no longer of use or value, then perhaps a person is justified in ending that life. The larger point is that even if we concede that life is a gift from God for which we should be grateful, the duty of gratitude is limited by considerations such as the property rights of the gift recipient, the utility or value of the gift, and so on. What proponents of the gift argument must prove is that despite the fact that God's gift of life makes our lives ours, we necessarily express ingratitude or disrespect by voluntarily ending our lives, regardless of how good or bad those lives are. I doubt such a proof is forthcoming.

To conclude this discussion of the religious arguments for the moral impermissibility of suicide, I believe that none of the three religious arguments analyzed here succeeds in showing that suicide is morally impermissible. Of course, proponents of these arguments may propose that they can be salvaged, that they may have been misunderstood, or that slight amendments to the arguments can make them sound. Yet if I am correct, the problems with these arguments do not stem principally from their being *religious* arguments; i.e., the problems do not result from the arguments resting on premises about God or the supernatural. Instead, the problems concern how the premises about God or the supernatural logically entail the conclusion that suicide is morally impermissible. In the case of the natural law argument, the problem is how claims about the natural purposes of human life are supposed to yield the conclusion that suicide is morally impermissible. In the case of the property and gift arguments, these arguments rest on analogies, and once unpacked, these analogies do not seem as strong as proponents of these arguments suppose them to be. Therefore, the religious arguments appear unsound simply because they are logically invalid, not because their premises are controversial.

Non-religious Arguments for the Impermissibility of Suicide

Let us now consider some arguments for the moral impermissibility of suicide that do not refer to religious premises.

The sanctity of life argument

One very popular argument for suicide's moral impermissibility is the sanctity of life argument. According to this argument, human life is intrinsically precious and valuable. Thus, human life as such is entitled to respect, even reverence. Killing human beings, including oneself, is therefore wrong because it fails to honor the intrinsic value of human life. The sanctity of life argument is popular because it expresses a simple and powerful moral truth that nearly everyone accepts: human beings deserve to be valued, and no action more clearly indicates that they are not valued than killing them. While this argument is sometimes put forth by religious thinkers, especially Catholics, it need not be grounded in a religious perspective at all.

The first question that should be posed about the sanctity of life argument is how willing its proponents are to accept the apparent consequences of their premise that human life is intrinsically valuable. On its face, this premise seems to disallow not only suicide, but also any killing of human beings, in any circumstance, for any reason. However, many people, even those who might be attracted to the premise that human life is intrinsically valuable, may still think that some killings *are* morally permissible. For instance, many people believe that abortion, capital punishment, or killing enemies in wartime is sometimes morally permitted. These are clearly controversial examples of morally justified killings, but other examples raise acute problems for the sanctity of life position. Suppose you are violently attacked by a gun-wielding criminal. Are you not morally permitted to use violence, even violence intended to kill your attacker, because your attacker's life is inherently valuable? Why doesn't the inherent value of your own life justify your taking his, however reluctantly? Or consider our earlier example from Chapter One: Foxhole Jumper. The sanctity of life view seems to imply strange or contradictory conclusions about Foxhole Jumper's jumping on the grenade. From one perspective, he gave his life in order to honor the intrinsic value of others' lives, yet from another, he probably foresaw that his jumping on the grenade would kill him, thus failing to honor the intrinsic value of his own life. Of course these descriptions are incompatible, implying both that Foxhole Jumper did and did not honor the intrinsic value of human life.

Some proponents of the sanctity of life argument may be willing to accept these implications of their view. Some Catholics, for instance, subscribe to the notion of a "seamless web of life," according to which all killing of human beings for any reason is morally impermissible. But notice that the sanctity of life view might also imply surprising things about our duties to keep people alive. If human lives are intrinsically valuable or precious, does this require that we take every conceivable measure to keep a person alive? Fortunately, all of the American astronauts who reached the Moon on the Apollo missions returned home safely. But imagine that one of the missions touched down on the Moon's surface, but upon attempting to depart, the astronauts discovered that their landing craft had been badly damaged and could not be launched back to Earth. Given the astronauts' oxygen supply, they might survive only a few days on the lunar surface. What are our moral obligations in such a situation? Do we have to bear any risk whatsoever that might save them? Advocates of the sanctity of life view seem to answer "yes," but you might have doubts. Yes, efforts to save them should be undertaken, but hard judgments would need to be made about which efforts are justified in light of the risks. For example, whether to send a second mission to retrieve the first set of astronauts is a gut-wrenching choice, but the thesis that human life in intrinsically valuable might imply that we should send a second mission because we should do everything possible to save the astronauts. Maybe so—but not obviously so. Or consider a more mundane example: many people approach the end of life under conditions where only very costly or very risky measures, such as surgery or very expensive radiological treatments for cancer, will keep them alive. As with the example of lunar astronauts, the choices here are difficult, and there is a voluminous literature in bioethics that hashes out the various alternative answers. Again, however, the sanctity of life view, if it implies that all measures should be taken to keep people alive, provides a simple answer. But you just might harbor the suspicion that such an answer is too simple.

To return to suicide: what do these counterexamples to the principle that killing human beings is always wrong have to do with suicide? They seem to show that the link between the premise that human life is intrinsically valuable to the conclusion that killing is always wrong is tenuous. If some killings are morally permitted, then the principle that all killings are impermissible is false. This might then lead us to ask why suicide (as self-killing) isn't sometimes also a permissible exception to this principle?

A second, and more direct, challenge to the sanctity of life argument is that human life simply is not intrinsically valuable. The Roman philosopher Seneca once remarked that because "mere living is not a good, but living well," the wise person "will live as long as he ought, not as long as he can."[1] Seneca's remarks call into question exactly what makes a human life valuable. Is it, as the sanctity of life view suggests, intrinsically valuable, valuable just so long as it exists? Or is the value of a human life dependent on the quality of a person's life? Many philosophers doubt that there is any value to a person's life that doesn't ultimately depend on the quality of a person's life: how happy a person is, how much pleasure a person enjoys, how much pain she suffers, how long she is likely to live, whether she will achieve her life goals, and so on. Certainly people make many important decisions guided by concerns about their quality of life. A person diagnosed with terminal cancer may have to choose between two courses of treatment: a regimen of chemotherapy and surgery that will extend her life but also involve pain and significant stretches of hospitalization, or a regimen in which pain or discomfort alone are treated but no more aggressive measures are taken to treat the cancer. The first option offers more life, but perhaps at a reduced level of quality; the second offers a shorter life, but arguably, a higher quality of life. Which one should the patient choose? Regardless of which she chooses, questions about quality of life are likely to be central to the patient's deliberation about her future. This suggests that when we are forced to think about the value of our lives, we tend to approach the issue in terms of the quality of life, not supposing that life (or being alive) is valuable in and of itself. Moreover, as critics of the sanctity of life argument have pointed out, if taken to its logical conclusion, the argument implies that the life of a person in a persistent vegetative state is intrinsically valuable simply because the person is biologically alive. But that sort of example seems to cast the sanctity of life view in an unflattering light.

Lastly, the sanctity of life argument is vulnerable to the criticism that it rests on an unintelligible moral duty. The argument claims that suicide is morally impermissible, and as such it violates a moral duty. An initial question to ask is to whom (if anyone) is this duty owed? One possibility is that the duty in question is owed to God. I will not make an explicit effort to show this here, but if the sanctity of life argument is meant to rest on a duty to God, then in all likelihood it is not a distinct argument but simply a different way of expressing the familiar religious arguments for the moral permissibility of

---

1   *Epistles* 70; see "On the Proper Time to Slip the Cable," trans. R.M. Gummere, in *Moral Epistles* (Cambridge: Harvard University Press, 1917–25).

suicide that we addressed earlier in this chapter. In other words, the sanctity of life argument will turn out to be a way of articulating the natural law argument, the property argument, or the gift argument, and it will therefore inherit all of the strengths and weaknesses of those arguments.

Perhaps the duty is not owed *to* anyone, but this is implausible. Sometimes we think of very general duties, such as the duty to promote happiness, as not really owed to anyone. The mistake here is to think that because such duties are now owed to *specifiable* individuals, they are thereby not owed to anyone at all. That is not the case however: we may have duties to individuals or groups answering to various descriptions that do not specify exactly who those individuals or groups are. We can have duties to whoever is driving the number 38 bus today, the human race, our unborn descendants, the applicants for the job, the people who end up unearthing this nuclear waste, and so on. But just because we cannot enumerate precisely who answers to these descriptions—because we cannot name every member of the human race, because we do not know who will apply for the job—it does not follow that these are not duties to others.

Another possibility is that the sanctity of life argument points to a duty to ourselves: that a suicidal person wrongs herself by ending her life. There are two difficulties with this proposal. The first is that, when it comes to our duties to others, very often acts that violate those duties become morally permissible if others consent to being treated in these ways. Rape is non-consensual sex; the other person's consent is what renders sex morally permissible. Similarly, my moral duties preclude me punching others in the face, but if a person agrees to a boxing match, then I do no wrong by punching my opponent in the face. Consent, then, often nullifies our duties to others, and if we apply that reasoning to suicide, it may follow that even if we have a duty, rooted in the "sanctity of life," not to end our lives, our consenting to suicide nullifies that duty. If so, then whatever the duty to self is that makes our lives sacred and would make suicide wrongful, this duty does not militate against suicide.

A deeper worry about rooting the sanctity of life argument in duties to ourselves is that many philosophers reject the notion that there even are duties to self. Some philosophers see morality as essentially social, concerned solely with how we treat others. According to these philosophers, while we can harm ourselves through ignorance, indiscipline, stupidity, etc., we never thereby *wrong* ourselves. Our only duties, then, are duties owed to others. I can hardly settle such a thorny theoretical question here. Many eminent philosophers, including Immanuel Kant, have defended the notion of duties to self,[1] whereas others think the duties to self are nonsense. Bernard Williams, for example, called such duties an "absurd apparatus."[2] But here is a simple way of motivating the thesis that there are no duties to self. Imagine being stranded alone on a desert island, so that you will never interact with another human being again and none of your actions will affect other human beings in the slightest. The only individual to whom you could have obligations is yourself. (Let us put aside the question of any moral obligations to animals and so on.) Do you have any moral obligations in such a scenario? If you answer "no," then you reject duties to self. If you answer "yes," then you must hold that there are duties to self. Again, the theoretical issues are too large to tackle here, but if the sanctity of life argument requires that there be duties to oneself, this is itself a controversial claim.

The social goods argument

Other non-religious arguments for the moral impermissibility of suicide are more explicit in claiming that the duty not to end one's life is a duty owed to others. One such argument I will call the social goods argument. This argument rests on the claim that suicide denies to the society in which a person lives the various social benefits of her continued living. Throughout our lives, we provide various goods to our society. We provide our labor, our expertise, and perhaps a moral example to others. Indeed, a society's continued existence depends on people providing these goods. If doctors stopped practicing medicine, if farmers stopped producing food, and if artists stopped creating objects for entertainment or enlightenment, a society would surely be worse off. Suicide clearly puts an end to a person's continuing to contribute these valuable social goods, so (according to the social goods argument) it is morally impermissible.

The social goods argument definitely gets one thing right: a society's existence and well-being *do* depend on the contributions made by its members. Problems arise, however, in trying to infer the moral impermissibility of

---

1   "On duties to oneself as such," *Metaphysics of Morals* (Cambridge: Cambridge University Press, 1993), pp. 173-77.
2   *Morality* (Oxford: Oxford University Press, 1972), p. 69.

suicide from such a premise. The premise itself, for instance, seems subject to limits. The social goods argument seems to imply that the reason we must stay alive—and hence, why suicide is morally wrong—is because each of us is obligated not only to support our society, but to give whatever we can to support our society. While the former claim seems reasonable, the latter does not. In fact, we routinely do not fault people for choices that result in their benefitting society less than they otherwise could. Professional athletes, street corner entertainers, and investment bankers benefit their societies, but probably not as much as school teachers, police officers, and emergency room doctors. Yet few of us criticize those who choose the former kinds of professions on the grounds that, had they chosen a more socially beneficial profession, their societies would be better off. In a similar vein, we do not criticize those who opt to retire and do nothing productive. Of course, people should be mindful of the benefits (and harms) that flow from such choices. Nevertheless, we are not obligated to maximize the social benefits of our choices. Note, though, that this pokes a hole in the social goods argument: suppose that we do owe our society some of the social goods we can provide, but we do not owe them all the social goods we might provide. If so, then those who have given *enough* social goods could commit suicide without violating their obligations to the larger society.

The social goods argument, then, does not appear to show that suicide is always wrong, even if we adopt the more plausible understanding of its premise, namely, that individuals have a limited moral obligation to support their societies. It might show that some suicides are wrong, for instance, suicides in which a person is about to bestow a great benefit on the larger society but kills himself in order to deny them that benefit. Imagine that Albert Einstein, instead of being a jovial guy, was actually very bitter and angry, and upon discovering the theory of relativity and appreciating its scientific implications does not bother to write down his findings but kills himself instead. Such a suicide would deny society (indeed, the whole world) a valuable social good. Yet notice that even here, it is not quite correct to say that angry Einstein's *suicide* denied the world his scientific discovery, since he could have failed to write it down and *not* ended his own life. This highlights another shortcoming in the social goods argument: the argument is most convincing when we have a clear picture of what social goods we'd be denying our society by killing ourselves. Suppose that several years earlier, a rather depressed Einstein commits suicide, before he would even have begun to think about questions in theoretical physics. Then it could be said that his killing himself actually *did* deny the world the scientific knowledge he might have produced had he lived. But observe "might": Einstein (nor anyone else, for that matter) may not have known that Einstein was headed for such a discovery. If that's the case, however, we may not be so confident in our own cases that we will be in a position in the future to provide our society various goods. The greater this uncertainty, the less emphatically we can say that a person who commits suicide denies her society the benefits of continuing to live.

The social goods argument also neglects an important fact: every member of society may well contribute to its well-being, but every member also imposes costs on that society. Every person must eat, be sheltered, and so forth. Some members of a society (children, the elderly, and the sick, for instance) are likely to be a net cost to a society, since the costs of keeping them happy and alive are higher than the value of the social goods they provide (and I do not mean to suggest that children, the elderly, and the sick do not provide social goods at all). But the observation that each of us is, to some degree at least, a cost to our society takes a bit of the sting out of the social goods argument. Suppose a person is very costly to society but can still provide some social goods of very modest value. The social goods argument still implies that such a person would act wrongly if she ended her own life, since she is thereby denying her society the social goods she might provide. However, this is a debatable conclusion: the wider the gap between the costs a person imposes on her society to keep her alive and the social goods she provides, the less credible it seems to say that such a person must stay alive. For what the social goods argument appeals to is the well-being of a society, and if a person is a significant net drain on her society's net resources and goods, can the proponent of the social goods argument maintain (without contradicting her own argument) that such a person may not end her life of her own accord?

The reciprocity argument

A slightly different argument that nonetheless holds that suicide wrongs one's society is the reciprocity argument. Recall that the social goods argument said that it is impermissible to end one's life, because in doing so, one denies to society various goods it needs to survive and flourish. One reason to doubt the social goods argument is that it simply assumes that we have a duty to support our society, but how did this duty originate? We are born into societies without having any say in the matter, so how exactly do we end up with a duty to support the society we are part of, a duty strong enough (according to the social goods argument) to disallow our killing ourselves? The reciprocity argument answers these questions by claiming that we may not end our lives, because in doing so, we wrong the society that made our own lives possible. The notion of reciprocity is that a person owes those who benefit her. What does a person owe her society in return for these benefits? According to the reciprocity argument, a person owes her society her labor, the fruits of her talents, and so forth. Since suicide denies a society these things, it is morally impermissible in that it violates a person's duty of reciprocity to her society.

It may not be easy to see how the reciprocity argument and the social goods argument differ. Even though both think that what renders suicide morally impermissible is that a person's suicide denies her society important goods, they differ concerning the underlying rationale for why it is wrong for a person to deny her society these goods. In the social goods argument, the existence and success of society is taken to be a good state of affairs, and hence something that a person ought to support, much in the same way that other people's happiness, being a good state of affairs, is something a person ought to support. In the reciprocity argument, a person ought to support the existence and success of society in exchange for the various goods society has provided, and her support for that society disallows her ending her life prematurely.

Yet despite this difference in their rationales, one of the objections leveled earlier against the social goods argument can also be leveled against the reciprocity argument. Surely there must be some limit to how much a person must give back to her society as part of her duty of reciprocity, and once that limit is met, the reciprocity argument no longer seems applicable. At a certain point in life, a person has probably "given back" all that is necessary in order to have met her obligation of reciprocity to her society. An aged person, for instance, may have contributed a great deal to societal welfare over the course of her life. Is there not a point at which she has satisfied her obligation to society and can do with her life what she pleases, including ending it if she so desires?

A second objection to the reciprocity argument is that sometimes the society itself fails to keep its end of the reciprocal relationship. Consider a young African American born in the US Jim Crow era, when the overwhelming majority of African Americans were relatively poor, had few if any recognized rights, were routinely treated cruelly or dismissively, and in some cases could even be subject to extralegal violence such as lynching. It is a kind of bad joke to think that such a person could not permissibly engage in suicide because doing so would prevent her from contributing to the society that gave so much to her. In fact, her society gave very little to her at all. Thus, her society did little to keep its end of the implicit bargain envisioned in the reciprocity argument. Yet if that is the case, then she does not owe them much in the way of reciprocity, and so presumably the suicide of such a person would not violate any duty of reciprocity she owes to her society.

The role responsibilities argument

A slightly different non-religious argument is the role responsibilities argument. Each of us has ties to various other people: we are employers or employees, parents or children, members of communities, and so forth. Suicide, on this argument, precludes us from fulfilling the responsibilities associated with these roles. A parent, for example, who takes her own life fails to fulfill certain moral responsibilities toward her children, including feeding and clothing them, ensuring their physical health, participating in their education, etc. So according to the role responsibilities argument, suicide is an indirect wrong, in that it makes it impossible for a person to fulfill the moral responsibilities she has toward specific other individuals.

It is important to see that the role responsibilities argument is quite similar to the social goods argument. Both arguments appeal to the thesis that suicide prevents us from fulfilling moral duties we have toward others. The arguments differ concerning who these duties are owed to and the nature of the duties. The social goods argument thinks of suicide as denying a large number of people some very general goods, such as one's labor. The role responsibilities argument thinks of suicide as causing very specific harms to very specific people. A parent's suicide may harm his children in very specific ways. So too can an entrepreneur harm her business partner, or a key member of a workplace harm his co-workers, via suicide.

This argument thus brings much of the ethical discussion surrounding suicide back down to earth: rather than framing the ethics of suicide in terms of duties to God or to that nebulous entity called "society," the role responsibilities argument reminds us that suicidal people are not isolated, but love and are loved by others. To have a loved one die by suicide is often a painful experience that can probably not be adequately captured in terms of the abstract talk about duties, rights, and so forth. The role responsibilities argument thus gives moral traction to the powerful sense of anger or abandonment that the loved ones of those who die by suicide often feel.

To its credit, the role responsibilities argument probably does show that *some* suicides are morally impermissible. The challenge is determining where the line is with respect to morally permissible and morally impermissible suicides. Role responsibilities vary from person to person, both in the sheer number of such responsibilities a person has and in how much others rely upon a person fulfilling those responsibilities. For instance, it is plausible to think that a parent with several young children who ends her life has done them wrong, because she has very significant role responsibilities toward them. Young children, after all, depend on their parents for many crucially important goods, such as food, shelter, emotional development, affection, and so on. Furthermore, it is difficult to find someone to provide these goods in lieu of parents. At the other end of the spectrum, some people have few, if any, ties to others and, consequently, few if any role responsibilities toward others. Consider the elderly widow with no children or siblings, for instance. Or, similarly, the vagabond bachelor who spends his life voluntarily riding the rails, traveling from region to region and living out of a rucksack, probably has few responsibilities. In such cases, it may be hard to see how, if these individuals were to commit suicide, they would be failing in any role responsibilities. But if the parent with several young children runs afoul of her role responsibilities, making her suicide morally impermissible, and the elderly widow or the itinerant bachelor have too few role responsibilities to render their suicides morally impermissible, what about the vast number of cases that lie between these extremes? As we have seen, we can probably identify some factors that might indicate where the line should be drawn by referring to the number of people toward whom a person has role responsibilities and the importance of the fulfillment of these responsibilities to others. In all likelihood, there is no unambiguous way to weigh these factors and determine exactly whose suicides are large enough violations of role responsibilities to make them morally impermissible.

Lastly, the role responsibilities argument must confront the issue of the individual's own well-being. How much suffering or unhappiness must a person tolerate in order to fulfill her role responsibilities? Again, there are no easy answers here, yet surely the well-being of the individual considering suicide cannot simply be disregarded but must instead be measured against the harms she may cause to family, friends, loved ones, etc. If so, then perhaps some suicides violate our role responsibilities, but when the harm or suffering of continuing to live is sufficiently great, our role responsibilities should take a backseat to relieving that harm of suffering.

The Kantian argument

A final argument for the impermissibility of suicide is the Kantian argument. (The argument is so named because it was first put forth by the eighteenth-century German philosopher Immanuel Kant.) Kant is a notoriously difficult philosopher to understand, so here I will attempt to express the core insights of the Kantian argument in as simple a fashion as possible.

The essence of morality, according to Kant, is that each person has what Kant calls "pricelessness" or "dignity." This means that individuals are valuable quite apart from the happiness they enjoy or bring to others. In fact, what makes an act wrong in this view is that it treats a person merely as a means to the happiness of someone else. Suppose that someone who made you a promise fails to keep it. Why is this morally objectionable? In Kant's view, promise breaking is wrong because it treats the person to whom the promise was made as an instrument or tool of the interests or happiness of the promise maker. As Kantians would put it, promise breaking treats the person to whom the promise was made as a mere means, instead of as an end in himself. Imagine that a friend borrows your car for a weekend vacation, agreeing to return it in time for you to drive to work on Monday. Yet she does not return the vehicle until Tuesday. Of course, your friend's broken promise is likely to cause unhappiness on your part, but Kant would locate what's morally wrong with the broken promise elsewhere. If your friend doesn't return the car in time, not only does she inconvenience you, she also treats your personal property (and by extension, you) as a resource or tool of her own aims. Kant does not deny that happiness is an important good, but what makes people valuable is their *autonomy*, their ability to guide their actions in accordance with their own choices. And in not keeping his promise, your friend interferes with your rationally chosen aims: you, after all, in agreeing to lend her your car for the weekend, trusted that she would return it in time for you to pursue your aim of going to work on Monday. In this sense, the broken promise thwarted your ability to fulfill your chosen aims, thus treating you as something less than the autonomous individual you are. (One way to appreciate the plausibility of this Kantian view is to modify the example somewhat: suppose the friend returns the car late, but has returned it with all its minor mechanical problems fixed, a full tank of gas, and a shiny new paint job. You are benefitted by her failure to keep her promise, but isn't her promise breaking still wrong despite its turning out to be beneficial to you?)

What bearing does Kant's view about autonomy have on the morality of suicide? Not only must we not treat other people's autonomy as a means to our own happiness, we must not treat our *own* autonomy as a means to our own happiness. But that, Kant says, is exactly what suicide often is: a person destroys herself, and thereby destroys the autonomous self that makes her have value or dignity, for the sake of her happiness (or more exactly, for the sake of putting an end to unhappiness). A person suffering from persistent depression, a painful illness, or a succession of devastating setbacks has understandable reasons to want end to her life, but to do so would be to destroy the autonomous self that gives our lives their importance. To take one's life because of the bleakness of the future is to reduce oneself to nothing more than a means for the realization of one's interests, or as David Velleman vividly puts it, to treat oneself "like a stick of dynamite, which realizes its nature by blowing itself up."[1] Suicide, in Kant's view, denies human beings the very dignity that makes them human.

The Kantian argument shares with the sanctity of life argument the notion that suicide is wrong because human lives are intrinsically precious and valuable. However, the Kantian argument is distinctive in that it is not the biological fact that someone is a living human that makes suicide wrong. Instead, what makes suicide wrong is the moral fact that human beings have autonomous rational wills that confer upon them dignity that cannot be traded in exchange for happiness, either their own or that of others.

There are many subtleties in Kant's views on suicide and self-destruction. For instance, Kant seems to hold that we do not have a duty to preserve our lives, and may even have a duty to end our lives, if doing so is necessary to fulfill some other duty. Indeed, sometimes Kant gives the impression that he thinks *all* suicidal conduct is motivated by a concern for one's own happiness. Certainly a great deal of suicidal conduct is motivated by self-interest in this sense. Our example Despondent, from Chapter One, is motivated to end his life because his future looks miserable. Kant would condemn such a suicide because Despondent treats his own autonomous self merely as a means to his

---

1   "A right of self-termination?" *Ethics* 109 (1999): 625.

future happiness (or more accurately, as a means to avoid future unhappiness). So too for many other suicides: they are wrong, in Kant's eyes, because they are motivated by what he would term self-love, a desire to realize one's own interests, but what about suicides that are not self-interestedly motivated— does Kant's view condemn those suicides as well? Recall Foxhole Jumper again. Far from seeming self-interested, Foxhole Jumper's suicide is the very antithesis of selfishness. He ends his life not for the sake of his own happiness but in order to make possible the survival of other autonomous beings, beings that (according to Kant) are priceless and have dignity. This is why, as I argued in Chapter One, Foxhole Jumper is perceived as courageous. How exactly Kantians should understand unselfish suicides is a complicated matter. Some argue that in an example like Foxhole Jumper, even though the soldier acts unselfishly in jumping on the grenade and even though his act saves the lives of intrinsically valuable humans, it is wrong because he treats himself as a mere means to the happiness of others. Other Kantians deny this and claim that by consenting to his own death, Foxhole Jumper is not treating himself as a mere means and his suicide is at least morally permissible. (Similar remarks might apply to the Spy example as well.)

But putting unselfish suicide aside for the moment, the more remarkable feature of the Kantian argument is that it denies that one's own happiness is ever sufficient moral grounds for suicide. Kant is in fact claiming that one's own happiness could *never* justify suicide—a conclusion that has struck some readers of Kant as incredible, even cruel. Try to envision the unhappiest person possible (someone stricken with a series of horrible misfortunes, a latter-day version of the Biblical Job). On Kant's view, this person may not permissibly end her life in order to end this unhappiness, no matter how awful or prolonged that unhappiness is. Even some philosophers otherwise sympathetic to Kant have found this conclusion repugnant.

The question then arises, where exactly does the Kantian argument go awry? Here are two possibilities.

First, some have suggested that Kant misunderstood the value of autonomy. In Kant's eyes, a person's autonomy is the source of her dignity, and it is incoherent to imagine that someone could be morally permitted to trade that dignity for anything else, even relief from severe and persistent unhappiness. We might say that Kant adopted a *narrow* interpretation of the value of autonomy: the fact that we are autonomous constrains what we may do to autonomous beings, including ourselves, and because of this, suicide is impermissible. Many Kantians, however, adopt what we could call a *wide* interpretation of autonomy. These Kantians remind us that autonomy is a capacity to make and be guided by our rational choices. Yet if an individual who, for instance, suffers from severe and persistent unhappiness rationally determines that she would be better off dead, why may she not permissibly exercise her autonomy by engaging in suicide? It is, after all, her life and her body, and it is difficult to see why, if she draws the reasonable conclusion that a shorter life is a better life, this runs contrary to the value of her autonomy. As the English philosopher John Stuart Mill would later put it, "Neither one person, nor any number of persons is warranted in saying to another human creature of ripe years, that he shall not do with his life for his own benefit what he chooses to do with it."[1] Some Kantians have thus concluded that Kantian moral thinking supports, rather than denies, a moral right to suicide in at least some circumstances.

A final objection to the Kantian argument is more direct: it simply is not true that the lives of some suicidal people are priceless or invaluable, as Kant claims. For those with truly miserable lives and bleak futures, it seems apparent that their lives are not valuable *to them*. Indeed, their lives seem more of a burden than a benefit. Of course, Kant may well reply that what is ultimately valuable about a person is her autonomy, which is still present even in people leading miserable existences. So even if a person's life is not valuable to her, it retains the dignity that, according to Kant at least, makes her valuable and makes it wrong for her to take her life. But here we might ask whether Kant's insights about the morality of how we treat others—that we are to respect their autonomy and not treat them simply as means to our own happiness—extend to how we treat ourselves. At the very least, it sounds strange to say that ending one's life always amounts to destroying that life in ways that treat it as mere means. There are kinds of conduct that treat ourselves as mere means: a person who sells herself into slavery does so, essentially making herself a tool or instrument of another person's happiness and denying herself her dignity. Yet at least some who consider suicide thoughtfully and rationally do not seem to be making themselves tools or instruments of anyone's happiness, including their own. They are determining that their lives are better if those lives are shorter, and Kant's claim that suicide is wrong because our autonomous selves are priceless simply does not seem to take that fact into account.

---

1   *On Liberty and Other Writings* (Cambridge: Cambridge University Press, 1989), ch. 4.

Conclusion

None of these arguments clearly and uncontroversially establishes that it is necessarily wrong for a person to end her life. At most, the social goods, reciprocity, role responsibilities, and Kantian arguments might show some suicides are morally impermissible, but none of the arguments supports the conclusion that suicide is necessarily wrong.

Note that these arguments are all concerned with the *morality* of suicide. They are not concerned with what we might call the *wisdom* of suicide, by which I mean, whether suicide is ever a wise or prudent decision. And it is wrongheaded to draw inferences about the morality of suicide from its wisdom: it could well be true that any given act of suicide, even if it is morally permissible, is nevertheless unwise or foolish, being motivated by false beliefs, bad evidence, etc. Just because a given act of suicide is morally permissible would not make that act a good idea in any larger sense.

Further Reading

The literature concerning arguments for the moral impermissibility of suicide is vast, so the following is only a small sample of this literature. Baruch Brody's anthology (2010) addresses many of these arguments from a historical perspective, as do Alvarez (1990) and Minois (1999). Battin (1996) considers many of these arguments, and many of the classic sources of these arguments (including excerpts from works by the Stoic philosophers Seneca, Aquinas, Hume, and Kant) can be found in Donnelly (1998).

David Hume's "Of Suicide," published in 1783 and now widely anthologized, is the classic critique of the natural law position on suicide. Gay-Williams (2011) provides a contemporary defense of that position. The Baron d'Holbach offers the classic criticism of the reciprocity argument in his eighteenth-century essay The System of Nature, or Laws of the Moral and Physical World; Holley (1989) analyzes the property and gift arguments, as does Beauchamp (1992).

Roberts and Wasserman (2009) outline the current state of the philosophical discussion about the non-identity problem.

Ronald Dworkin (1993) defends a version of the sanctity of life argument. Peter Singer (1994) is a prominent critic of the sanctity of life argument on the grounds that quality of life is central to the value of a life.

I discuss and critique Kant's arguments for the impermissibility of suicide in Cholbi (2000, 2010). David Velleman (1999, 2008) defends a Kantian stance on the ethics of suicide in his writings.

three

The Moral Permissibility of Suicide

Thus we hear that suicide is the most cowardly of acts, that only a madman would commit it, and similar insipidities; or the senseless assertion that suicide is 'wrong', though it is obvious there is nothing in the world a man has a more incontestable right to than his own life and person.[1]

THE LAST CHAPTER CONSIDERED a wide range of arguments supporting the conclusion that suicide is morally impermissible. Though moral attitudes and beliefs about suicide continue to vary greatly both within and across cultures, it is fair to say that at least in Western nations, moral attitudes and beliefs about suicide have been trending in a more permissive direction for the past several centuries. Suicide is almost never legally prosecuted nowadays, despite the fact that it remains a crime in many parts of the world, and a number of nations now legally sanction assisted suicide under specific

---

1   Arthur Schopenhauer, "On suicide," in *Essays and Aphorisms* (New York: Penguin, 1973), p. 77.

circumstances. Various factors serve to explain these increasingly permissive attitudes: a decline in the influence of traditional religions, greater appreciation for the suffering caused by the mental illnesses associated with suicide, longer lifespans, and deeper societal commitment to personal liberty.

Yet from a philosophical perspective, our concern is not simply in documenting changes in moral attitudes or beliefs, but in determining whether such changes in attitudes are justified. In this chapter, then, we will critically examine several arguments aimed at showing that suicide is morally permissible. Before doing so, however, we must confront the thesis that no argument is necessary for suicide in order to conclude that suicide is morally permissible.

Must a Permission Be Justified?

Philosophical issues are sometimes framed by the questions we ask in connection with them. For example, when philosophers discuss the issue of free will, they typically take as their central question "do human beings have free will?" To those who believe we do have free will, the very framing of this issue in this way may appear prejudicial. By asking whether we do have free will, the question appears to assume either that human beings do not have free will or that there are sufficiently strong reasons to doubt human freedom that we need arguments to overcome those doubts. Hence, making this question central tilts the debate about free will in one direction. If, on the other hand, the issue of free will were addressed principally by considering a question such as "is human behavior outside our control?", then perhaps the debate would unfold in ways that are more congenial to the thesis that we do have free will. These remarks illustrate that how a philosophical issue is approached can often affect where we understand the *burden of proof* to lie. By taking a certain question as central to philosophical inquiry into a particular subject, we may inadvertently (and perhaps incorrectly) assume that arguments must be given in favor of a thesis in order for us to accept that thesis, rather than its being the case that arguments must be given against a thesis in order for us to reject it.

Philosophers attracted to *antinatalism* are prone to detect an unfair assignment of the burden of proof in discussions of the moral permissibility of suicide. Antinatalists vary in their exact philosophical commitments, but they share the beliefs that human life is not good, that those who are born are not benefitted by being born, that to be born is to be wronged, and that existing human beings have an obligation not to reproduce. Arthur Schopenhauer is perhaps the best known historical antinatalist, and David Benatar is its chief contemporary spokesperson.[1] For antinatalists, existing human beings have no moral obligation to continue to exist. After all, those human beings had no choice in the matter concerning whether to exist, and their existence is not a benefit to them. Antinatalists are likely to see the demand for arguments showing that suicide is morally permissible as a reflection of natalist bias, i.e., a bias in favor of living and continuing to live. Does not the fact that we consider such arguments at all indicate an implicit, but wrongheaded, assumption that suicide is, without an argument to the contrary at least, morally *impermissible*? By critically addressing arguments for suicide's impermissibility, we may seem to be tilting the scales against the permissibility of suicide in the first place. As the antinatalist Sarah Perry, who blogs under the pseudonym "Sister Y," writes, to frame debates about the morality of suicide in this way essentially mandates "that it is the suicidal person who must justify his refusal to live, rather than the community being required to justify the action of forcing him to live."[2]

Where should the burden of proof lie, then, in debates about the morality of suicide? Should those who believe suicide is morally wrong have to provide arguments for their thesis, or should it be those who believe suicide is at least sometimes morally permissible? In general, those who believe an act is morally impermissible bear the burden of proof, not their opponents; that is, we typically demand arguments or reasons why an act is wrong instead of arguments or reasons why it is not wrong. An act's being morally permissible is the "default," we might say, and further arguments or reasons need to be provided to show either that an act is morally impermissible or morally required. It is difficult to say why we assume that an act's being permissible is the default. I suspect that this assumption reflects a factual probability: few acts are morally impermissible or required, the overwhelming majority are simply permissible, and so the likelihood that any act selected at random is neither required nor impermissible is great. Therefore, given the likelihood that any particular act is morally permissible, we should, for the purposes of moral inquiry, assume its permissibility. But regardless of the source of this assumption, it seems clear

---

1   *Better Never to Have Been* (Oxford: Oxford University Press, 2008).

2   "An introduction," View from Hell weblog, 23 March 2008 (http://theviewfromhell .blogspot.com/2008_03_01_archive.html).

that, just as in the law, in moral matters we assume that our acts are innocent until proven guilty.

Given this common assumption, the complaint that searching for arguments for the permissibility of suicide clandestinely assumes suicide's impermissibility needs to be taken seriously. And in my own defense, I concluded in the last chapter that there is no uncontroversially sound argument for the impermissibility of suicide, thus indicating that I have some sympathy with the assumption that suicide is also innocent until proven guilty—that arguments need to be offered for the impermissibility of suicide rather than for its permissibility. But there are two grounds for thinking that in the case of suicide, perhaps those who believe suicide is permissible do bear the burden of proof, thus making it reasonable to seek out and assess arguments for the permissibility of suicide.

The first is that those who believe the moral permissibility of suicide should be assumed without argument appear to be drawing a false inference from the contrary thesis. Recall Perry's suggestion that it is misguided to assume "that it is the suicidal person who must justify his refusal to live, rather than the community being required to justify the action of forcing him to live." Implicit in this critique is the supposition that unless suicide is morally permitted, a community is justified in "forcing" a suicidal person to live. We will delay careful discussion of the ethics of suicide intervention and prevention until Chapter Five, but for now it suffices to note that it does not follow directly from the premise that suicide is morally impermissible that forcing a suicidal person to live is morally permissible. In fact, it is not obviously true that we are morally permitted to force others to do what they are morally obligated to do. (My neighbor may have an obligation to save money for her children's college education, but it is not obvious that I am morally permitted to force her to save her money!) Nor does it follow from the premise that suicide is morally permissible that forcing a suicidal person to live is morally impermissible. For it is not obviously true that morality prevents us from compelling others to do what it is nevertheless morally permissible for them not to do. (Perhaps drivers are not *morally* obligated to wear a seatbelt, but many people think it quite reasonable for the law to compel them to wear a seatbelt anyway.) In any event, no simple inferences can be drawn from the moral status of suicide to the moral status of efforts to prevent suicide.

The second reason to suppose that the moral permissibility of suicide needs a justification stems from the most salient moral fact about suicide:

it is a species of killing. The philosopher who saw this most acutely was the Christian apologist St. Augustine. He was among the first Christian thinkers to defend the claim that suicide is morally impermissible, and he did so in a clever way. As a pious Christian, Augustine understood the Bible as God's word, indeed, as the final word on ethical questions, and in a famous discussion of the Ten Commandments, Augustine wrote that

> The law, rightly interpreted, even prohibits suicide, where it says "Thou shalt not kill." This is proved especially by the omission of the words "thy neighbor," which are inserted when false witness is forbidden in the commandment."[1]

Augustine argues, in other words, that suicide is morally impermissible because it amounts to killing a person, and if God had intended to exempt killing oneself from His command not to kill, He would have made it explicit in the way that He made explicit that one is not to covet another person's spouse.

I concluded in Chapter Two that the religious arguments for moral impermissibility are at best controversial and none is obviously sound. I mention Augustine's discussion of the morality of suicide, not in order to revisit those arguments, but to highlight a problem that any philosopher, whether religiously inclined or not, who is interested in the morality of suicide needs to confront: granting the obvious difference between suicide—self-killing—and homicide—killing another person, is there an important *moral* difference between them?

Here is an example to make this question clearer: Rachel and Sarah are twin sisters, both of whom have been diagnosed with incurable forms of cancer. In neither case is the prognosis good: each is expected to live about one year, and though palliative care will diminish their suffering, Rachel and Sarah face the prospect of significant pain prior to death. After three months, Rachel and Sarah find themselves in adjacent beds at a hospice. Rachel decides that she cannot bear the prospect of continued life and plans to commit suicide by injecting herself with an overdose of tranquilizers clandestinely acquired and smuggled in by her son. However, before administering the lethal dose of tranquilizers, Rachel crawls out of her bed and injects a sleeping Sarah with a

---

1   *City of God Against the Pagans*, trans. B. Dombart and A. Kalb (Cambridge: Cambridge University Press, 1998), book I, chapter 20.

similar dose of tranquilizers. Rachel then injects herself. Rachel and Sarah are dead within ten minutes.

Rachel's killing Sarah is homicide. Rachel's killing Rachel is suicide. Is either act morally permissible? Those who think suicide needs no moral justification are apt to say that Rachel's suicide is morally permissible. But why should that be? After all, seemingly the only salient difference between Rachel's killing herself and Rachel's killing Sarah is who is killed. And if (as seems reasonable) Rachel's killing Sarah is morally objectionable, then her killing herself should be equally objectionable. Put bluntly, why should the fact that suicide is killing *oneself* exempt it from the general moral prohibition on killing? After all, almost everyone accepts that killing human beings is a serious moral wrong, maybe even the most serious such wrong. So why, for instance, ought we to think that Rachel's killing herself belongs in a different moral category from her killing Sarah?

Here is a slightly different, but illuminating, way to think about Augustine's reasoning. In order to justify treating two people differently, we need to identify some morally important difference between them. A judge can justifiably sentence one convicted arsonist to a harsher sentence than another arsonist if there is a morally important difference between the two criminals or their crimes. Differences of this kind could include that the first arsonist had committed previous crimes and thus displays worse moral character; that the first arsonist set a fire that knowingly put human life in danger; or that the first arsonist set his fire during warm, windy conditions that made his act more reckless. Returning to Augustine's reasoning: is the fact that in suicide the person one kills is oneself, whereas in homicide the person one kills is someone else a morally important difference sufficient to show that the former is less morally objectionable than the latter?

My worry is that those who think suicide needs no moral justification do not take seriously enough the fact that suicide is a species of killing, and insofar as killing is in general a serious moral wrong, it needs a compelling justification. It will not do to simply dig in our heels and say that what morally differentiates suicide from homicide is that suicide kills the person who engages in it. As we established in Chapter One, that is merely a fact about what suicide *is*. But what seems necessary is an argument as to why that fact is morally salient—why the fact that suicide is self-killing makes it morally different from killing another. Yes, suicide is not homicide. But since both involve the apparent moral wrong of killing, how is suicide morally distinct from homicide? That suicide is self-killing is not a moral claim sufficient by itself to indicate whether suicide is morally permissible.

Thus, just as we dissected arguments for the moral impermissibility of suicide in the previous chapter, in this chapter we will dissect arguments for the moral permissibility of suicide. This is not because it is apparent where the burden of proof lies with respect to the morality of suicide. Instead, it is precisely because it is *not* apparent that we need to consider arguments on both sides. And, intriguingly enough, the arguments for the moral permissibility of suicide are not flawless either.

Self-defense

Let us begin with a very clever argument for the moral permissibility of suicide, one that questions whether suicide is fundamentally different from *permissible* homicide.

Many people think that the prohibition on killing others is not absolute. For example, many people clearly accept that killing enemy soldiers in the course of waging war is morally justified. Capital punishment, the killing of those guilty of certain especially heinous crimes, is thought, in some quarters, to be another example of justifiable homicide. However, both war and capital punishment are highly complex and controversial ethical matters, and there is hardly a consensus that these are examples of morally justified homicides. But there is one kind of homicide that many people believe is morally acceptable: killing in self-defense. If, in order to prevent another person from killing us or causing us grievous bodily harm, we must kill that person ourselves, such a killing would, in many eyes, be morally justified.

There is a vast ethical literature exploring self-defense and a great deal of philosophical disagreement about how best to explain why killing in self-defense can be morally justified. However, suppose we simply grant for the sake of argument that killing in self-defense is sometimes morally justified. How might this provide an argument for the moral permissibility of suicide? If some acts of suicide sufficiently resemble acts of self-defense, then perhaps there is *not* a morally significant difference between such suicides and killing others in self-defense. Put differently: if the very same reasons that justify killing another person in self-defense also apply to some acts of suicide, then those acts of suicide are morally justified too. So rather than trying to identify a fundamental moral difference between suicide and homicide, this appeal to self-defense puts suicide and homicide more on a moral par by pointing to an apparent moral *similarity* they may have when they are morally justified.

The obvious puzzle here is to make sense of *suicide* as an act of self-defense. Suicide is self-killing. How can killing oneself also be defending oneself? And against what might one be defending oneself against by ending one's life? Let us consider examples of what many people would intuitively consider morally justified suicides and see if they can be justified in terms of acting in self-defense.

Suppose that a person suffers from a persistent and painful medical condition. The condition in question could be cancer or AIDS, or a mental disorder such as depression. In such a situation, it is understandable that a person might judge that her life is no longer worth living and that, on the whole, her interests are better served by shortening her life through an act of suicide. Can suicide be justified as an act of self-defense in this case? Is it true, for example, that a person who concludes that her existence subject to the ravages of such diseases would be so painful could defend herself against this harm by killing herself in self-defense?

Here are reasons for skepticism. We sometimes say that conditions such as cancer or depression "attack" us, much in the way that the flu virus attacks us, and that such an attack should be answered or repelled by treatment. But self-defense is most naturally understood as defending oneself against something that exists independently of the self. Viruses and other disease-causing microbes survive in other people or organisms and in other environments. Thus, the existence of these entities does not depend on us. This is not the case for incommunicable conditions such as cancer or depression, however. There are not "pieces" of cancer or depression in the world seeking hosts. These conditions are *endogenous*: they originate within the person who suffers from them. In contrast, viruses are *exogenous*: they can (and do) exist outside us and cause harm to us only once they enter our bodies. Therefore, if acting in self-defense requires acting against something exogenous to ourselves, then a person who ends her life due to the sufferings associated with conditions such as cancer or depression is not acting in self-defense. Thus, such suicides could not be justified in terms of self-defense.

However, perhaps this is the wrong way to understand suicide as an act of self-defense. Perhaps the threat a person defends herself against by committing suicide is not something distinct from us in a physical or metaphysical sense but is instead distinct from us in an ethical sense. In other words, in killing herself, a person sometimes destroys a force that precludes her from living in a way that is consistent with who she believes she is or ought to be. The philosopher Peter Raabe elaborates this insight, saying that suicide can involve "choosing the evil of an *authentic* death (in which the act of ending one's own life is in one's own hands) over the evil of an *inauthentic* life (in which others have the power to dictate and control one's life)."[1] These others who dictate and control one's life could be other people, but perhaps more abstractly they could also be conditions that a person does not see as defining or characterizing who they are or what they care about. A person debilitated by the pain of long-term cancer or another disease may see the cancer as an intruder in her life, as something that prevents her from being who she fully is or would most like to be. The inability to pursue her career, to develop her talents, to practice her hobbies, to take pleasure in what once was pleasurable, to be as engaged with the lives of her loved ones—all of these are obstacles to living the life she might otherwise choose for herself. The life of the depressed individual or the cancer patient is thereby inauthentic. Such a person might see death, in contrast, as the lesser evil when compared to living a life that is inauthentic, that does not reflect one's nature or concerns. To end one's life is thus a way of living more authentically by exercising control over one's death. Here is Raabe again:

> In other words, as self-defense, suicide is an act believed to counteract these external forces.... It is meant to counteract the annihilation of the self, to prevent the total loss of self-image … and to preserve what little remains of personal dignity and self-respect. It is the last desperate act of a struggle to retain, albeit in self-annihilation, some semblance of power and control over oneself.[2]

Raabe provides us with the most fully elaborated way of seeing suicide as an act of self-defense. However, even conceding that suicide may sometimes be an act of self-defense in the manner Raabe proposes, I am reluctant to endorse his radical conclusion that "suicide *cannot* be immoral when it is an act of

---

1   "Suicide as self-defense," in *Issues in Philosophical Counseling* (Westport, CT: Prager, 2002), p. 174; emphasis in original.

2   Raabe, p. 174.

self-defense."[1] Granting that homicide is sometimes justified as an act of self-defense, it is less apparent that suicide can be easily justified in such terms.

First, this appeal to self-defense is ambiguous concerning what exactly is defended in an act of suicide. In killing oneself in order to prevent living an inauthentic existence, one in which one is controlled by a force external to one's own values, one does not thereby preserve this authentic self. The self, in both its authentic and inauthentic guises, is destroyed. Admittedly, suicide ensures that a person will not live inauthentically, but it does nothing to ensure that a person lives authentically. Suicide, according to this self-defense argument, avoids the evil of inauthenticity but does not realize the good of authenticity. Ironically, then, Raabe may thus be correct in calling suicide a "hopelessly paradoxical achievement."[2] A person striving not to living inauthentically avoids that fate through an act which, by its very nature, precludes living authentically.

More worrisome still is that suicide in self-defense turns out to be a misnomer. Whatever makes self-defense morally justified turns on the insight that to be harmed or killed by another person's aggression is unfair, thus making it reasonable to defend oneself. But suicide in self-defense doesn't end up defending the person who is under attack from disease, disability, depression, or the like. When a cancer patient receives chemotherapy to "defend" herself against her cancer, the intent of the treatment is to destroy the cancer and ensure the patient's survival. But when that same patient kills herself, claiming that she is acting in self-defense to prevent her authentic self from being destroyed, she not only destroys the cancer, she destroys herself in the process. The self under threat is not defended at all; it is destroyed.

Furthermore, part of what seems to justify self-defense in ordinary cases is that the individual who attacks us does not pose a threat to us merely due to coincidence. The attacker whom we might kill in self-defense is more likely to be an aggressor who seeks to harm us, rather than, say, an innocent toddler who stumbles toward us with a loaded gun. Here philosophical opinion splits, but many argue that what entitles us to act in self-defense is not simply the presence of a threat to our well-being, but the presence of an *aggressive* or *deliberate* threat to our well-being. On this view, attacking or killing the toddler may well be wrong because although the toddler poses a threat to us, the

---

1   Raabe, p. 175; emphasis added.
2   Raabe, p. 175.

toddler does not seek to harm us and is not acting aggressively. The toddler's death would be undeserved. In contrast, an aggressive attacker, someone who seeks to do us deliberate harm, may be attacked or killed precisely because the threat he poses to us stems from his aggression. He is not an innocent attacker. What, then, of suicide in "self-defense"? In cases where disease threatens us, we would be killing ourselves in self-defense. But note that in acting in self-defense against ourselves, we are, like the aforementioned gun-toting toddler, innocent attackers. Thus, if self-defense is permissible only against "guilty" at-tackers, suicide in self-defense would not be permissible. Here the self is more like an innocent bystander, an individual whom (most writers on self-defense would agree) it is not morally permissible to kill even in the face of a terrible threat such as cancer.

Lastly, we might wonder what is so terrible about living under the control of a condition that alienates us from our existing values or identity. Many people appear to be "hung up" on a certain conception of who they are: typi-cally, the conception of themselves as competent and independent adults at the peak of their cognitive, physical, and emotional capacities. But life is not simply a story that culminates in this period of peak competence and inde-pendence and then proceeds downhill from there. For large stretches of our lives, we are not fully competent or independent. We are, instead, vulnerable, dependent, or in need. Such is the case in childhood, during periods of pro-longed illnesses, and (often) in old age. The process of aging or undergoing physical decline could be seen not as a threat to one's authentic self but an opportunity for personal growth, as a chance to fashion a new set of values or concerns in light of the bodily changes that have occurred. At the very least, it is far from obvious that a person is prevented from living an authentic life or a life consistent with values they can endorse if they are under attack by depression or cancer.

The appeal to self-defense, if sound, would show that some instances of suicide are justified in exactly the same way as some instances of homicide: as acts of self-defense. However, the parity between killing others in self-defense and killing oneself in self-defense, even under this revised ethical sense of self-defense, does not withstand scrutiny.

Self-knowledge

A second argument for the permissibility of suicide appeals to the premise that each of us knows our own interests or well-being much better than others do. Rachel's suicide is permissible, this approach might say, because she alone knows and appreciates her plight sufficiently to determine whether ending her life reflects her interests or well-being. Hence, a central condition for her self-killing being morally permissible is met. However, Rachel is not in such a privileged position with respect to Sarah's well-being or interests. Only Sarah, one could argue, is in a position to know enough about her well-being or interests to know whether her dying reflects her interests or well-being. Hence, the moral difference between Rachel's permissible suicide and her impermissible killing of Sarah is that Rachel has enough knowledge of her own well-being or interests to justify the former but not the latter. More generally, suicide is more often morally permissible than homicide because suicide is the killing of the only person ideally situated to know whether dying reflects his or her interests or well-being: the person who dies. To kill someone else, on the other hand, would require a similar level of knowledge concerning that person's interests or well-being, which we do not have.

As we shall see, this approach will not justify the permissibility of suicide. Nevertheless, it does contain an important insight. We are intimately aware of ourselves in ways that others are not. For example, others can often know that we are in pain by observing our grimaces and so on, but only we ourselves are directly aware of this pain. More broadly, it seems reasonable to assume that we ourselves know what tends to give us pleasure or cause us pain, what gratifies and satisfies us, what we fear and what we seek. Yet this claim should not be exaggerated: our interests and well-being are not fully transparent to ourselves. It is not unusual, after all, to discover that we are mistaken about our own wants and desires. One need not subscribe to the idea of a Freudian unconscious to recognize that people are often uncritical about their own interests or well-being, going long stretches of their lives organizing their lives around wants and desires they assume they care about only to discover later that their true wants and desires lie elsewhere.

Worse still, when it comes to a decision as important as ending one's life, it seems especially crucial not simply that a person probe her *current* wants and desires, but that she be able to project her *future* wants and desires as well. As the philosopher Richard Brandt points out:

The person who is contemplating suicide is obviously making a choice between future world-courses: the world-course that includes his demise, say, an hour from now, and several possible ones that contain his demise at a later point.... The basic question a person must answer in order to determine which world-course is best or rational for him to choose, is which he would choose under conditions of optimal use of information, when all of his desires are taken into account. It is not just a question of what we prefer now, with some clarification of all the possibilities being considered. Our preferences change, and the preferences of tomorrow are just as legitimately taken into account in deciding what to do now as the preferences of today.[1]

Do suicidal people fully and accurately take into account their future wants and desires when considering whether to end their lives? We human beings are prone to short-term thinking in any case, but the frequency with which suicidal thoughts are associated with mental illnesses such as depression raises additional red flags, for one of the defining symptoms of depression is a tendency to have not only a negative image of oneself, but also an irrationally pessimistic (or even nihilistic) view of the future. Thus, depressed individuals may often lack a clear enough sense of their desires, current or future, to be in a position to rationally determine whether suicide advances their interests or well-being. (As we shall see, this fact has far-reaching implications concerning both the moral justifiability of such suicides and how others may intervene to prevent suicides.)

If it is far from obvious that human beings, especially those prone to suicide in the first place, know enough about their own well-being to determine if suicide reflects their interests or well-being, then it might be assumed that other people do not have such knowledge (or are at least less knowledgeable than the individual considering suicide). But this assumption is not necessarily valid. It seems likely that given how depression distorts individuals' thinking concerning their own well-being, other people, such as a mental-health professional or a loved one, may have a much better understanding of a depressed person's overall well-being than he himself does. Parents, for instance, are likely to have a better understanding of their children's interests

---

1   "The morality and rationality of suicide," in S. Perlin (ed.), *A Handbook for the Study of Suicide* (Oxford: Oxford University Press, 1975), p. 69.

or well-being than do the children themselves. Thus, this reasoning—that suicide is more often morally permissible than homicide because individuals themselves have adequate knowledge of their own interests and well-being that others lack—rests on an arguable matter of fact.

Yet even supposing this factual claim were true, this appeal to self-knowledge would still not provide a moral defense of suicide. Even if it is true that we always, or nearly always, have sufficient knowledge of our own interests or well-being to know if suicide is in our interests, this is no argument that suicide is in our interests. Imagine that Hector has sufficient knowledge of his well-being to know *if* suicide is in his interests. It follows neither that suicide *is* in his interests nor that suicide *is not* in his interests. All we know is that *Hector* knows which one of these is true. A comparison: a competent doctor knows whether a patient's symptoms point to the patient having pneumonia. But his competence does not determine whether the patient has pneumonia. His being able to figure out if the symptoms point to pneumonia is rather what makes him a competent doctor. In other words, the doctor, being competent, knows which of these are correct:

(1) The patient has pneumonia.
(2) The patient does not have pneumonia.

But whether (1) or (2) is true is logically independent of the doctor's competence or judgment. Similarly, having enough knowledge of one's interests to know whether suicide is in one's interests is probably a necessary condition of a suicide being rational. But having such self-knowledge tells us nothing about what it is that a person knows.

Upon analysis, this approach also has extremely counterintuitive implications concerning homicide. Return to our example of Rachel and Sarah. Assume that Rachel really does have enough knowledge of Sarah's situation and her well-being to know whether ending Sarah's life would be in Sarah's interests. The *absence* of such knowledge might be a reason against Rachel's killing of Sarah being justified. But few would accept that the *presence* of such knowledge in Rachel is a reason that justifies her killing Sarah. (To put it in more exact logical terms: knowing that death is in a person's interest can be a necessary condition of that person being justifiably killed, but it is never a sufficient condition.) Homicide, after all, is not an act we would ordinarily excuse on the grounds that the killer knew enough to know that his victim's interests are served by dying. Similarly, whether Sarah should die (or more properly, be killed) is up to Sarah, we might say, even if others know well enough whether she should die.

Finally, those who morally oppose suicide are likely to point out that the self-knowledge argument rests on an unstated, and debatable, premise. Suppose we assume that if a person with self-knowledge of her interests determines that suicide is in her interests, then suicide is in her interests. Her suicide being morally permissible does not follow unless we make the additional assumption that any suicide that is in a person's interests is also morally permissible. But this assumption, as we have seen, could be rejected from a number of different angles. Those who reject suicide on religious grounds may deny that suicide, even if in a person's interests, is morally permissible. They would counter that such suicides still destroy God's property, express ingratitude to God for the gift of life, etc. Defenders of the sanctity of life argument may argue that suicide wrongfully destroys something sacred, even when suicide is in the person's interests. Kantians oppose any suicide that is self-interested, and those who argue against suicide because of its effect on others are likely to say that the interests of the suicidal person must be considered alongside the interests of others. In short, then, the self-knowledge argument simply assumes, without additional argument, the premise that suicide is not wrong unless it fails to be in the individual's interests. But that premise is clearly a controversial one.

At most, then, the argument appealing to self-knowledge shows that the rationality, and perhaps the moral permissibility, of suicide might hinge on a person having sufficient knowledge of her own interests to know that suicide is in her interests. But its failures show that what is required is a claim that somehow implies that we have a special *moral* relationship to ourselves that we do not have with others, the sort of relationship that protects others from killing them but gives ourselves wider latitude in killing ourselves.

Self-ownership

In Chapter Two, we considered a well-known religious argument for the moral impermissibility of suicide: the property argument. This argument claimed that because we are God's property, it is wrong for us to destroy ourselves through suicide. As we noted, this argument is problematic on several counts.

However, the notion of property also plays a role in an argument for the moral permissibility of suicide. Instead of God owning us, this argument claims, we own ourselves. Our bodies are our property, and just as with anything else we own, we have the right to do with our bodies what we please. I own the laptop computer used to write this book, and because I own it, I am morally permitted to treat it in certain ways. I can improve it by adding additional software to its hard drive or by painting colorful designs on its case. I can sell it if I determine it no longer meets my needs or if I purchase another laptop. And if I so desire, I can even throw it in the trash. The same is true of anything else that is my property, including my own body. I can improve my body through physical exercise, surgery, or (arguably) tattoos. Some would argue that I am morally permitted to sell my body (or at least parts of it, such as my blood or my kidneys). And if the circumstances appear to me to warrant it, I can do to my body the equivalent of throwing my laptop away: I can destroy my body through suicide.

To its credit, the property argument for the moral permissibility of suicide does rest on an apparently significant moral asymmetry, that of self-ownership. If it makes sense to say we own anything, it appears to make sense to say not only that we own our own bodies, but also that we do not own other people or their bodies. We therefore have a special moral relationship to ourselves that we do not have to others, a relationship that (it would seem) could justify destroying ourselves but not justify destroying others. In addition, as I have already noted, the property argument makes sense of the moral permissibility of a good many other things we do to our bodies. We can opt to improve our bodies, though of course that also implies a right to mistreat our bodies through bad health habits, for example. Some arguments for the moral permissibility of abortion appeal to this very idea of a woman owning her body.

Yet this argument suffers from two flaws. The first is that its conclusion is necessarily a limited one, since destroying one's property is not morally permissible when it causes harm to others or puts them at risk. Suppose that I destroy my car by packing the front seat with dynamite and then exploding it. Such an explosion could harm bystanders, put others' property at risk of fire, emit toxic fumes, and so on. Because my car is my property, it is morally permissible, in general, for me to destroy it. However, not every *way* of destroying it is morally permissible, and in particular, I may not destroy it in ways that cause great harm or risk to other people or to their property. Similarly, even if my body belongs to me as a piece of property, it is possible for me to destroy that body in ways that violate obligations to others, including the obligation not to subject them to harm or the risk thereof. Moreover, as we noted in our discussion of the role responsibilities argument in Chapter Two, some suicides are harmful to others or violate our obligations to them. Hence, even if the self-ownership argument makes a convincing general case for the moral permissibility of suicide, it cannot justify any and all suicides.

The second flaw with the self-ownership argument is more damning. The notion that we own our own bodies may seem uncontroversial, but a moment's reflection suggests that this is a more puzzling notion than we might expect. That we can own alarm clocks, teddy bears, or stock options is clear enough. In owning these things, they belong to us. But it is harder to conceptualize how *our* bodies belong to *us*. First of all, how do we come to own our bodies? With other property items, we can typically identify how we came to have ownership over them: we found them, bought them, or created them through our labor, for example. But none of these holds true of the body. We did not exist at a certain point and then come to own our bodies. Rather, our supposed ownership of our bodies temporally coincides with our own existence. Our bodies came to exist at the moment we came to exist. On top of that, we do not seem to be able to treat our bodies in the ways we can treat other things we own. For instance, we can physically distance ourselves from our property and it remains ours. If I leave my house one morning, my house does not cease to be my property while I am gone. But not so with my body, for it is not even clear how I could leave my body behind and go somewhere else. Furthermore, we can entrust our property to others. I can ask that my neighbor feed my dog or water my plants while I am on vacation, and if she agrees but fails to come through, I have a right to complain.

But in what sense can I entrust my body to someone else? Perhaps when I agree to be anesthetized in preparation for surgery, I am entrusting my body to the care of my doctors. While it is true that I am letting them see to my welfare while I am unconscious, the analogy with entrusting my property to others is inexact at best. For it is not true that while I am anesthetized, I (or my body) is going elsewhere. My body is still there but is in an unconscious state. Lastly, it is doubtful that a person's body can be sold in the usual sense. Usually, in a sales transaction, an item is transferred *from* the seller *to* the buyer at the moment of sale: I receive money for my laptop and transfer physical possession of the laptop to you. But that seems impossible in the case of my body, for I cannot transfer my body to another person, since there is not anything that remains after I transfer my body to another person. In transferring my body, I am transferring *me* to another person. Granted, perhaps I can sell, and thereby transfer, my labor to another person, as when I become someone's employee. Yet that is clearly not the same as transferring myself to another person.

Behind these worries is the fact that the notion of self-ownership is incompatible with certain features of property ownership. In particular, a person's owning something is only possible if that something is not the person; that is, property ownership is necessarily ownership of something that is not oneself. If this is right, then the notion of self-ownership—that my relationship to my body is one of property ownership—is facially incoherent.

Advocates of the self-ownership argument may offer two replies to these objections. First, they may point out that these objections assume a particular view of our relationship to our bodies, namely, the naturalistic view that we are, or our existence of mental beings depends upon, our bodies. But there is another view of our relationship to our bodies. According to the dualistic view, our mental life resides in a non-material mind or soul whose existence does not logically depend on our bodies. From this perspective, the mind or soul continues to exist even after the body is destroyed. If correct, this view could make better sense of the notion of self-ownership by postulating that the non-material mind or soul owns the body and can decide to destroy it just as it could decide to destroy any other property it owns.

I readily concede that the dualistic view can make sense of the notion of self-ownership, yet in some cases the solution to a philosophical problem is more troubling than the problem itself. Dualism may indeed be a more troubling hypothesis than the incoherence of self-ownership. For, as I noted in Chapter Two, dualism is a controversial, even dubious, view of the relationship between our minds and our physical bodies, and it is intellectually perilous to defend a controversial thesis against criticism by invoking an equally controversial thesis. If accepting dualism is the cost of making sense of the notion of self-ownership, that cost may well be too high.

A second response to these objections runs as follows: to deny self-ownership implies that our bodies are the property of someone else. But this is wrong—and morally troubling as well. We are not others' property, and the idea that our bodies are owned by others is morally alarming. Hence, we should accept self-ownership because the alternative answer to the question of who owns our bodies is even less plausible.

The obvious problem with this response is that it too overlooks an alternative: perhaps our bodies are not best thought of property at all; perhaps no one, neither we nor anyone else, owns our bodies. This response assumes that our bodies are property and must therefore be owned by someone, but this is an undefended assumption. Those invoking self-ownership clearly intend to defend the thought that suicide is morally permissible because we have a certain liberty over our lives. But as we shall see below, self-ownership is not the only possible route to defending such a liberty.

Autonomy and Rationality

A final argument harkens back to our discussion of Kant and autonomy in Chapter Two. Recall Kant's notion that as human beings we have autonomy, the ability to guide our actions in accordance with our own choices. I noted that Kant's notion of autonomy is understood in different ways, and according to what I there called the wide interpretation of autonomy, autonomy gives people a right to choose when their lives will end. Contrary to Kant's own way of deploying autonomy, autonomy licenses rather than prohibits suicide. In 1997, a group of philosophers submitted a legal brief to the US Supreme Court in conjunction with two cases concerning physician-assisted suicide. Their brief expresses well this autonomy-based rationale for suicide:

> Each individual has a right to make the most intimate and personal choices central to personal dignity and autonomy. That right encompasses the right to exercise some control over the time and manner of one's death.[1]

To see how this invocation of autonomy could make suicide morally permissible, let us return to our original example of Rachel and Sarah. Rachel, we might say, is autonomous with respect to herself. She has the right to choose to end her life, and so her own suicide is morally permissible. However, Rachel is *not* autonomous with respect to Sarah. Sarah has the right to exercise her autonomy to make the "intimate and personal" choice of ending her life, but

---

1   R. Nozick et al., "Assisted suicide: The Philosophers' Brief": "Conclusion," *New York Review of Books* 27 March (http://www.nybooks.com/articles/archives/1997/mar/27/assisted-suicide-the-philosophers-brief/).

Rachel does not. Hence, the fact of autonomy establishes the very asymmetry needed to justify suicide: suicide is less morally objectionable than homicide because suicidal persons are permitted to exercise their autonomy with respect to themselves.

The autonomy argument for the permissibility of suicide has been widely influential. This is not surprising, since it appeals to values that most of us hold dear: self-determination, individual conscience, and so on. Yet this argument is not without its shortcomings. For it is doubtful that "*each* individual has a right to make the most intimate and personal choices central to personal dignity and autonomy." For example, children should not be given the right to make such choices. Indeed, it is difficult to imagine *any* situation where a child's suicide is morally permissible, and it is not hard to see why: even granting that children are autonomous, they are not (in general) *rationally* autonomous. As we noted in our discussion of the self-knowledge argument, suicide is rational only when the suicidal person has sufficient knowledge of her own well-being or interests. But children are not especially good judges of their own well-being or interests. Left to their own devices, most children would avoid school, eat candy, and forego inoculations against infectious diseases. In addition, children seem to lack the rational capacities associated with acting appropriately on their judgments. Children are typically more emotionally volatile than adults and are often challenged by situations demanding self-control. Both of these are types of irrationality: children often lack sufficient knowledge of their well-being or interests and often lack the capacity to guide their behavior in accordance with their well-being or interests. Therefore, children do not meet an important condition for a suicidal act to be morally justified.

The example of children suggests that a more persuasive autonomy argument should appeal not to autonomy as such, but to *rational* autonomy. Why is rationality an important ingredient in the exercise of autonomy? A full investigation of this question would require a more thorough analysis of rationality and autonomy than we can undertake here, but here are some insights that might explain why it is rational autonomy, rather than autonomy alone, that matters to the moral justification of suicide. In a trivial sense, all suicides are autonomous, since they are acts in which a person does something to herself. But the mere fact that a person causes her own death does not show that she does what she herself desires to do. For one thing, as we saw in Chapter One, a person can cause her own death without desiring or intending it. Moreover, the link between our actions and our desires is tenuous, even fragile. In some cases, our long-term desires are overwhelmed by more immediate ones, as when a man committed to eating a healthier diet cannot resist the unhealthy snacks available at parties and at his workplace. In other cases, our ignorance of how to fulfill our desires results in acting in ways that hinder rather than advance our desires. A woman who seeks a career that uses her communications skills may wrongly choose a career as a scientific field researcher. In still other cases, we seem fundamentally ignorant of how our actions result from desires that we fail to recognize, and in so doing are not acting on desires we can acknowledge as our own. A man abandoned by his mother at a young age may not understand how these events result in powerful desires not to commit fully to a romantic partner. In all these cases, individuals end up acting on desires that are not their own. I do not mean by this that they act on someone else's desires; rather, I mean that the desires that in fact motivate their choices and actions are not always those they would want to motivate their actions.

In these cases, it is doubtful that a person is acting autonomously because he does not seem to be acting as he would if his actions reflected what he most fully desired. Let us say, then, that it is at least a necessary, and possibly sufficient, condition for a suicide to be morally permissible that the individual in question be exercising her rational autonomy in choosing to die. We have already seen that there are strong reasons to doubt that children are rationally autonomous, and therefore their suicides are not morally permissible. The larger challenge to the autonomy argument is that many others besides children might not meet this condition either.

To appreciate why, remember that we have some idea of what it would be for a suicidal act to be autonomous: for it to be self-chosen, rather than being coerced, imposed by someone else, or something similar. But exactly what more must be added to an autonomous suicidal act to render it rational? Most philosophers would agree with Glenn Graber's remark that a person's suicide is rational when "a reasonable appraisal of the situation reveals that one is better off dead."[1] More specifically, two general features must be present in order for a suicidal act to be rational. The first is that the suicidal person must exhibit appropriate cognitive functioning. Broadly speaking, this means that all of the mechanisms and mental systems by which a person acquires her

---

1   "The rationality of suicide," in S. Wallace and A. Eser (eds.), *Suicide and Euthanasia: The Rights of Personhood* (Knoxville: University of Tennessee Press, 1981), p. 65.

beliefs and desires are functioning soundly. Among these mechanisms and mental systems are a person's sensory capacities (her vision, hearing, etc.); her ability to reason about what she perceives, making appropriate inferences, etc.; her possession of a largely realistic worldview, one uninfluenced by paranoia, superstition, and so on; and adequate information relevant to the rationality of her suicidal act (for example, in the case of a patient with a terminal illness, how long she will live, the severity of pain she may suffer in the future, etc.). So long as a suicidal individual meets these cognitive conditions, she is supplied with an important ingredient in deliberating rationally about whether to kill herself: she is likely to have beliefs that reflect her actual situation.

In addition to these cognitive conditions, most philosophers propose that a suicidal act is rational only if certain interest conditions are met. Margaret Battin has suggested two such conditions.[1] The first is that the person's suicide is less harmful to the person than continuing to live. This condition being met thus hinges not only on how harmful it would be for the person to continue to live (how much suffering, hardship, etc. her future life would portend), but also how painful her death would be and the benefits she would enjoy in her future life. A young person could fail to meet this condition if, for instance, she was suffering from a painful but treatable medical condition and had a long, worthwhile life to look forward to should she continue to live. Second, Battin argues that a suicidal act must accord with a person's fundamental interests and commitments. By this she means that the suicidal act must reflect the sorts of values that a person holds most dear. A lifelong religious person who believes that his life is in God's hands—that God will and should decide the manner and timing of his death—would not be acting on his fundamental interests or commitments by committing a suicidal act. Similarly, a person who values her children's welfare might not be acting in accordance with her fundamental interests and commitments were she to end her life and thereby abandon her young children.

Note that the relationships between these two kinds of conditions, and between these conditions and autonomy, are complex. First, a suicidal act may be cognitively rational but not rational from the standpoint of a person's interests. (The examples given in the previous paragraph could be of this type.) Likewise, a decision concerning whether to continue living or to end

1   *Ending Life: Ethics and the Way We Die* (Oxford: Oxford University Press, 2005), p. 115.

one's life might meet the interest conditions without the person being cognitively rational. It could, for instance, be the case that a suicidal person who is mentally deranged might be better off dead. Presumably, her derangement would prevent her from rationally appreciating that she is better off dead. This highlights an important difference between the two kinds of conditions. The cognitive conditions are conditions of the suicidal individual, having to do with her mental attributes and abilities. The interest conditions, in contrast, are conditions of the individual's choice, having to do with what the individual chooses to do. Because we tend to assume that anyone who is not cognitively disordered will in fact act in his rational self-interest, and vice versa, we may overlook the possibility that these conditions can come apart. Moreover, notice that these conditions operate in concert to make autonomy possible, but they do not ensure that a suicidal act is autonomous: a person whose suicidal act meets these conditions is choosing to do (since the cognitive capacities she deploys are functioning adequately) what she has most reason to do (based on *her* fundamental interests and commitments). However, even these two conditions are not sufficient for a suicidal act to be autonomous. Consider our example of Rachel and Sarah again: Sarah could well meet the cognitive and interest conditions, since her cognitive function could be adequate and her dying could be in her considered interests while enabling her to avoid future harm. However, when Rachel kills her, she does not choose her own death. Thus, strangely enough, her suicide may well have been rational without being autonomous. A rationally autonomous suicide must therefore be one in which an individual not only meets both the cognitive and interest conditions, but also, on the basis of her adequate understanding of her situation, values, and future, rationally chooses to end a life that is not, on the whole, worth living any longer.

Is suicide irrational?

So if a suicide is justified only if it is rationally autonomous, then are suicidal acts rational? As with many matters surrounding suicide, generalizations are dangerous, so we had best proceed slowly.

Let us begin with the cognitive conditions. As we have noted, suicidal behavior is strongly correlated with mental disorders such as depression and bipolar disorder. However, these disorders influence mood, rather than cognition, and for the most part, those who suffer from the disorders correlated with suicidal behavior do not exhibit cognitive irrationality. They are not delusional, prone to illogical thinking, and so forth. (In fact, the phenomenon known as "depressive realism" suggests that depressed individuals may be *abnormally* cognitively rational.) There are exceptions, of course. For instance, a suicide undertaken while under the influence of mood- or cognition-altering drugs would almost certainly fail to meet the cognitive conditions. In addition, in certain instances of what are called dyadic suicides, an individual ends her life motivated by a desire to produce a certain reaction in others. For instance, the suicidal individual may hope to insult another person, cause them sorrow, or exact revenge. The person both desires to be dead and desires to be alive in order to experience others' reaction to her death. Such suicides are irrational when the individual is so fixated on this motivation that the finality of death, and the fact that she will not actually be around to experience the desired reaction, is forgotten.

A second worry is that suicidal thinking is sometimes triggered by crises or stressful situations that tend to distort our thinking. For some suicidal individuals, their preoccupation with dying is sparked by a specific stressor, such as a professional setback, the end of a romantic relationship, or the death of a loved one. Such evidence produces powerful emotions, including grief, loneliness, or anger. The psychologist Brian Mishara has concluded that the decisions made under these circumstances are highly emotional and highly volatile because these forms of mental anguish compromise our ability to deliberate rationally.[1] In 2009, a New Jersey teenager committed suicide after being victimized by persistent cyber-bullying in which his classmates spread rumors about his sexuality on the Internet. For highly sensitive individuals, such events undoubtedly cause stress that distorts their otherwise rational thinking. Such events coincide with the finding that suicidal individuals, especially those with mood disorders, view their perceived options narrowly and struggle to identify ways to alleviate their suffering. The mood disorders, depression in particular, thus appear to exert influence on individuals' patterns of thinking, rigidifying it and quashing their ability to imagine a better future for themselves.

These examples of apparently irrational suicide are limited to fairly specific individuals and circumstances. Yet are there reasons to think that suicide is, in

---

1   "Suicide types," in R. Kastenbaum (ed.), *Macmillan Encyclopedia of Death and Dying* (New York: Macmillan, 2010), p. 647.

general, cognitively irrational? Phillip Devine has argued that because no one knows for certain what happens to us after we die—whether, for instance, our conscious minds continue to exist after death—suicide cannot be rational.[1] I do not share Devine's skepticism. I am fairly confident that our conscious minds, because they depend for their existence on the continuing operation of the physical brain, do not continue to exist after death. Yet his conclusion highlights a legitimate, and more far-reaching, worry about the rationality of suicide. Suicide ends one's life: do those contemplating suicide comprehend this fact adequately? Doubtless, nearly every suicidal person *knows* that her action is likely to result in her death, but it is useful here to distinguish simply knowing something to be true from *appreciating* its truth. To know a fact is to stand in a particular cognitive relationship to it, to acknowledge or recognize its truth. But to appreciate a fact is to stand in a particular evaluative relationship to that fact, to know why that fact is important and to utilize that fact appropriately in her subsequent thinking. Thus, a person can often be said to know a certain fact without actually appreciating it. For example, I may tell a friend that I received a 1952 Willie Mays baseball card as a birthday gift. After I relate that fact to my friend, he knows it. But he may not appreciate it because he does not know other facts which, if known, would convey the significance of this fact. He may not know, for instance, that Mays is my favorite player or that the 1952 card, being his rookie card, is rare and expensive. He knows that I received the card, but he does not fully appreciate the significance of that fact. This example suggests that appreciating a fact, as contrasted with merely knowing it, can involve knowing other facts with which it is logically related and which explain the significance of that fact. In other instances, lack of relevant experience can block appreciation of a fact. Suppose that my neighbor is a renowned connoisseur of fine wine and tells me that he recently tried a vintage whose nose reminded him of Beluga caviar. I have never tried Beluga caviar, and in fact have almost no experience with the taste of caviar. For me, the comparison of the wine's nose to Beluga caviar simply fails to register. Since I trust my neighbor's expertise in wine tasting, I could be said to know that the wine's nose suggests Beluga caviar. Yet I do not appreciate that fact, for I do not quite know what it is that I know. My own lack of experience with the relevant facts precludes my understanding the significance of the

---

1   "On choosing death," in *The Ethics of Homicide* (Ithaca, NY: Cornell University Press, 1978).

comparison. Hence, we can fail to appreciate a fact when our inexperience blocks an understanding of that fact's significance.

Recall that among the cognitive conditions a suicidal act must meet are that the person must possess the ability to reason about what she perceives, making appropriate inferences, and that she must have adequate information relevant to the rationality of her suicidal act. These conditions bear a close relationship to what we have described here as "appreciating" the fact that suicide results in one's own death. A rationally autonomous suicide is not simply one where a person knows she will die. It is one where she knows what she is doing; that is, she makes use of the facts she knows in order that she can make rational decisions in light of those facts. She must, in other words, appreciate the fact that suicide leads to death, not simply know it. Without this appreciation, the relevant facts do not guide her decision making in the right way. Therefore, her choice about whether to continue or to end her life is not a rationally autonomous one.

Many suicidal persons, though they know their actions will lead to their own deaths, do not appreciate that fact. Certainly, they know their actions will end their lives; indeed, that is the very point of suicide, and suicidal persons typically have at least a partial appreciation of that fact. They appreciate, for instance, that suicide will bring to an end the pain or suffering that is motivating them to consider ending their lives in the first place; thus they appreciate the positive significance of their own deaths, but they seem often not to appreciate the negative significance of their own deaths. A parent may know, but not appreciate, that death will separate her from the children she loves. A business executive may know, but not appreciate, that his death will preclude him from enjoying future success in his ventures. This tendency to fixate on the positive significance of death instead of on its negative significance—to appreciate the former but not the latter—is especially troubling given the close relationship between suicidal thoughts and mental illnesses such as depression. Depression encourages just this sort of lopsided appreciation of the positive significance of death over its negative significance. It produces despondent moods that fix the sufferer's attention on hardships or suffering, accentuate the sufferer's sense of helplessness, and reinforce self-blaming patterns of thinking. Furthermore, depressed people tend to discount the value of the future; that is, they assign far less importance to possible future happiness, however remote, than they do to present or immediate suffering. This is in fact a common tendency among human beings in general, but it is especially pronounced among the depressed.

Serious questions, then, can be raised about whether suicide is cognitively rational if being cognitively rational demands an appreciation of death. There is truth, then, in the claim that suicidal people do not really know what they are doing.

Having considered the cognitive conditions, let us turn briefly to the interest conditions. Recall Battin's two interest conditions: a suicide is rational only if dying prevents more harm than it causes and if it accords with the suicidal individual's fundamental interests and commitments. As we noted earlier, the cognitive conditions and the interest conditions are independent of one another, so a suicide that meets one set of conditions does not necessarily meet the other, and vice versa. However, this is compatible with the conditions being related to some extent, and in this case, it is likely (though not necessary) that suicidal acts that do not meet the cognitive conditions also do not meet the interest conditions. And this is what we should expect: those whose thinking about their own deaths is rationally distorted are likely to reach erroneous conclusions about how much they have to lose from suicide, how much they have to gain from it, the suffering it may cause friends and loved ones, how it fits with their larger values and life plans, etc. Furthermore, the fact that suicidal thinking is often recurrent but not persistent (i.e., most suicidal people have more than one episode where they seriously contemplate suicide but do not contemplate it constantly) suggests that when suicidal individuals opt to die, they do so somewhat capriciously, without taking due account of all the consequences of their decision. Thus, there is substantial overlap between suicidal acts that do not meet the cognitive conditions for rational suicide and those that do not meet the interest conditions for rational suicide. And since, as I have argued, many suicidal acts do not meet the cognitive conditions, nearly as many suicides do not meet the interest conditions either. The Scottish philosopher David Hume was therefore almost certainly mistaken in asserting that "no man ever threw away life while it was worth keeping."[1]

To recap: the autonomy argument for the moral permissibility of suicide is successful only to the extent that suicidal individuals are rationally autonomous. But because there are legitimate doubts about whether most suicidal individuals meet the cognitive or interest conditions for a suicidal act to be rational, there are therefore legitimate doubts as to whether suicidal acts are

---

1   "Of suicide," in *Dialogues Concerning Natural Religion and Posthumous Essays* (Indianapolis: Hackett, 1998).

rationally autonomous. As a result, the autonomy argument is not obviously sound either. This should not lead us to believe, however, that every suicidal act is irrational. But it should at least establish a presumption that any given suicidal act probably is, thus placing the burden of proof on those who claim a given suicidal act is rational.

Conclusion

The arguments considered in this chapter—the self-defense argument, the self-knowledge argument, the self-ownership argument, and the autonomy argument—do not appear to be straightforwardly sound arguments for the moral permissibility of suicide. If I am right about this, and if the conclusions of Chapter Two are correct, then the dialectical situation concerning the ethics of suicide is dizzying but fascinating: there do not appear to be any sound general arguments either for the moral impermissibility of suicide or for its moral permissibility.

Further Reading

The "Philosophers' Brief" was submitted to the US Supreme Court as commentary on *Washington v. Glucksberg* and *Vacco v. Quill* and was published in the *New York Review of Books*. Richard Brandt (1975) initiated a great deal of the contemporary debate about the rationality of suicide. Battin (1996) outlines her cognitive and interest conditions for rational suicide; her account resembles Graber (1981). Joel Feinberg (1978) addresses the self-ownership argument. Peter Raabe defends his view of suicide as self-defense in Raabe (2002). For an argument that suicide simply cannot be categorized as either rational or irrational, see Cowley (2006).

four

Is Suicide Ever a Duty?

None of us get to write the final chapters of our lives as if we had nothing whatso-ever to do with other people.[1]

RECENTLY, PHILOSOPHERS HAVE DISCOVERED (or perhaps re-discov-ered) a different, and arguably more troubling, ethical question concerning suicide: is there ever a duty to commit suicide? Is it ever the case, in other words, that a person who does *not* kill herself thereby does something that is morally wrong? In my experience, many find this possibility unsettling. As we will see, the notion of a duty to commit suicide raises hard philosophical questions, but on a more direct and personal level, there are clear reasons why we might find the possibility of a duty to commit suicide to be troubling. For one thing, a duty to commit suicide raises the stakes higher than the debates described in Chapter Two. Suppose, for example, that after reading that chapter, you conclude that none of the arguments, whether secular or religious, shows that suicide is necessarily wrong. What follows? Only that there are some circumstances in which suicide is not wrong, that is to say, that suicide is morally permissible in some circumstances. Yet it definitely does not

---

1   Howard Brody, *Stories of Sickness*, 2nd ed. (Oxford: Oxford University Press, 2002), pp. 256-57.

follow that continuing to live is *ever* morally impermissible, and to the extent that we can imagine ourselves ever desiring to commit suicide, it may be more difficult to imagine ourselves being convinced that we have a duty to die. We might think that only a person with an inadequate appreciation for life would think she had a duty to bring her life to an end. And of course, even if we were convinced we had a duty to die, our natural fear of death would probably cause us to fear acting upon that duty.

"Is suicide ever a duty?" thus pushes us beyond issues of whether we *may* end our lives to issues of whether we sometimes *must* end our lives. My purpose here is to address whether the arguments given for a duty to commit suicide are sound.

Clarifying a "Duty to Die"

Unfortunately, discussions of whether suicide is morally obligatory are often couched in terms of a "duty to die," and the phrase "duty to die" is apt to mislead us. In particular, to propose that someone has a duty to die in a certain set of circumstances might lead us to overlook that the duty in question is not a duty to die *per se* but a duty to die so as to fulfill some other moral duty. In other words, the duty to die does not appear to be a fundamental duty but rather a duty, in certain circumstances, to bring about the end of one's life because dying (or at the very least, risking one's life) is the only or the most effective way of fulfilling a more fundamental duty. Take, for instance, the well-known real-life example of Captain Lawrence Oates, who many philosophers believe had a duty to die. Oates was a member of a 1912 Antarctic expedition, during which he became ill. It is likely that if Oates had continued on the expedition, his presence would have burdened his companions. The weather conditions the expedition confronted in Antarctica—not a hospitable environment for human beings in any case—were severe, and the expedition began to run short on supplies. Had Oates continued on, he might have consumed scarce resources, with little assurance that he would survive even with those resources, and delayed the expedition, thus putting the other members at risk.

Many philosophers have concluded that Captain Oates had a duty to die. (You need not be completely confident in that conclusion in order for me to make my point here.) And in fact, Oates could be said to have fulfilled this duty, since he decided one evening to leave his tent, abandoning the expedition and never to be found again. Suppose for the sake of argument that Oates had a duty to die. If so, why? First, had Oates stuck with the expedition, he might have subjected the other participants to a greater risk of dying. It would have been selfish, even reckless to do so. In general, we have a duty not to subject others to such risks. But as with most any duty, there are limits to what morality can ask of us in the service of that duty. A classic example of a duty that is limited in its demands is the duty to rescue. The philosopher Peter Singer has made famous the following "drowning boy" scenario:

> To challenge my students to think about the ethics of what we owe to people in need, I ask them to imagine that their route to the university takes them past a shallow pond. One morning, I say to them, you notice a child has fallen in and appears to be drowning. To wade in and pull the child out would be easy but it will mean that you get your clothes wet and muddy, and by the time you go home and change you will have missed your first class.
>
>   I then ask the students: do you have any obligation to rescue the child? Unanimously, the students say they do. The importance of saving a child so far outweighs the cost of getting one's clothes muddy and missing a class, that they refuse to consider it any kind of excuse for not saving the child. Does it make a difference, I ask, that there are other people walking past the pond who would equally be able to rescue the child but are not doing so? No, the students reply, the fact that others are not doing what they ought to do is no reason why I should not do what I ought to do.[1]

Singer puts the "drowning child" scenario to other argumentative purposes, but he also acknowledges that although it is clear that there is a duty to rescue the child, this duty may be limited by circumstantial factors. If, for instance, the child were drowning not in a shallow pond, but in a raging seastorm, then jumping in to save the child might well be foolhardy, ending in the deaths of both the child and the rescuer. In those circumstances, the duty to rescue appears to be overridden by the risks that rescuing poses to the would-be rescuer.

---

1   "The drowning child and the expanding circle," *The New Internationalist* April 1997 (http://www.utilitarian.net/singer/by/199704—.htm).

This illustrates that many duties are limited and, more specifically, that many duties are limited by the harm that fulfilling them would cause us. If this is so, then it is likely that the duty to die might be limited in precisely the same way, so that the duty to die must be weighed against the harm caused to the person whose duty it is. This suggests a first principle for how we should assess a duty to die:

> *Weightiness Principle*: A person has a duty to die only if, in the circumstances in which she has this duty, her dying would fulfill a basic moral duty the expected value of whose fulfillment is significantly greater than the expected value of any harms that may befall the person as a result of fulfilling this duty.

We can see how the Weightiness Principle makes sense of the apparent limits on the duty to rescue: saving the drowning child undoubtedly has great expected value in comparison to the harms of getting wet and muddy, but jumping into the raging seastorm puts something of very great value—the rescuer's life—at risk.

A second principle concerning the duty to die can also be illustrated in the tale of Oates. In that case, dying appeared to be the only course of action that would enable Oates to fulfill this duty. If the expedition party had unexpectedly come upon a hospital or the expedition's doctor had magically cured Oates's illness, then Oates would not have needed to die in order to avoid subjecting his peers to great risk, in which case he would not have had a duty to die. Hence, in Oates's situation, there did not appear to be any alternative available to him, besides knowingly subjecting himself to the risk of death, that would have allowed him to fulfill his duty not to subject the remainder of the party to similar risk. This in turn suggests a second principle about the duty to die:

> *Means Principle*: A person has a duty to die only if her dying is, all things considered, the most efficacious means to fulfilling a basic moral duty.

Under the circumstances, Oates could not have fulfilled his duty in any other way short of producing his own death. Obvious though it may be, most of our duties are not best fulfilled by dying. I may have a duty to yield my front-row seat on the bus to a handicapped rider. I could kill myself and thus "yield" my seat, but that's far from necessary. However, the point behind the Means Principle is precisely that: a duty to die exists only when dying really is necessary in order to fulfill a basic duty.

In this chapter, we will investigate the question of the duty to die by considering four general kinds of examples where some would argue that an individual has a duty to commit suicide (or at least knowingly put themselves at risk of death): suicide in the service of a political or religious cause, suicide ordered by the state, suicide to remove burdens one is placing on others, and suicide to save the lives of others. Using both the Weightiness Principle and the Means Principle as tools of analysis, I will argue that only very rarely do we have a duty to die.

One last word on the concept of a "duty to die" before considering the four examples: I am here going to treat the notion of a "duty to die" as equivalent to a duty to intend one's suicide, with the caveat here that suicide should be understood in the sense proposed in Chapter One, as intentional self-killing. More specifically, the duty to die could be fulfilled through a wide range of causes or sequences of events. A person with a duty to die may, in certain circumstances, have a duty to take active measures to cause her own death. But a person may, in other circumstances, have a duty to forego what is necessary to sustain life (giving up one's share of scarce food so that others might live, perhaps). Or in other circumstances, the duty to die might amount to a duty not to resist another person's attempt to kill you (as when a spy refuses to give up vital state secrets even under the threat of death). In still other circumstances, the duty to die may amount to a duty to seek others' aid in dying (as in physician-assisted suicide). The larger point is that in each of these cases, the duty to die is a duty to intentionally bring about one's death, whether passively or actively, on one's own or with others' assistance.

Suicide in the Service of a Political or Religious Cause

Some of the most famous suicides in history have been those undertaken to advance a political or religious cause. One of the most famous news photos in history depicts the Vietnamese Buddhist monk Bồ Tát Thích Quảng Đức, who in 1963 set himself ablaze to protest the South Vietnamese government's persecution of Buddhists. Đức's protest suicide later served as a model for other anti-war protestors throughout the world. Indeed, some historians assert that Spartan soldiers undertook a suicide mission in their famous battle against the Persians at Thermopylae.

In asking whether there is ever a duty to die in the service of a political or religious *cause*, we are not asking whether people might sometimes take their lives for political or religious *reasons*. In medieval times, a large number of Jews committed suicide because they faced persecution at the hands of Christians. Likewise, slaves in the antebellum American South were known to end their lives, and it seems reasonable that at least some did so because of the despair caused by the injustices of slavery. However, I am interested in suicides undertaken specifically in order to advance a political or religious cause: suicides done in protest, to draw attention to the cause, to indicate devotion to the cause, etc. For even though some suicides may be due to political or religious reasons, it is unlikely that those suicides could be morally required. Recall that the duty to die is not a basic duty, but one resting on some more basic duty. Hence, we may ask this: if there is ever a duty to die in the service of a religious or political cause, what is the more basic duty that is fulfilled by the duty to die? Although this is vague, I would suggest that the duty in question must be a duty to promote justice or truth. In other words, those who commit suicide in the service of political or religious causes may be required to do so if doing so fulfills a duty to make the world a more just place, or if doing so promotes belief in the truth, for example, belief in the "true religion." That there is such a duty is of course a big philosophical claim, one that I will not bother to defend here, but it does seem like the most plausible candidate for a basic duty, the fulfillment of which would make sense of individuals' having a duty to die in the service of a political or religious cause.

So, assuming there is such a duty, is there ever a duty to die in the service of a political or religious cause? Let us consider this question in light of the Weightiness and Means Principles.

The Weightiness Principle compels us to examine the value of the duty fulfilled by suicides in the service of a political or religious cause. The most powerful reason to be skeptical about such suicides being morally required is that it is far from obvious when one's cause is morally legitimate, that is, when a person's death *in fact* serves the aims of justice or truth. Imagine that a young German in the 1920s was attracted to Nazism and believed that, through a dramatic suicidal act, he could help bring Hitler and the Nazis to power. Surely the young German did not have a duty to commit suicide, precisely because the cause he sought to advance was patently *un*just. This is a highly dramatic hypothetical example of a suicide undertaken in the service of an unjust political cause. But it illustrates the more central worry that since a duty to die in the service of a political cause seems to require that the cause be a just one, we have powerful reasons to second guess any suicide undertaken for such a cause. I am not a philosophical skeptic, but it does not take a skeptic to have healthy doubts about whether we know which causes are rooted in justice. What, after all, is a just world—or a just society? Those envisioned by Enlightenment thinkers? Those proposed by Marxists or socialists? Those embodied in the ideals of the ancient Romans or of warrior-era Japan? Needless to say, this book is not the place to pursue foundational questions of political philosophy, but the difficulty of such questions should give us pause in thinking about a duty to die in the service of a political cause.

The case of suicide to advance a religious cause is even more problematic. Especially worrisome is that people are regrettably susceptible to religious charlatans—and sometimes end their lives for the sake of such religions. In 1978, more than 900 followers of the Reverend Jim Jones took cyanide at Jones's urging. Jones told his followers that they were committing "an act of revolutionary suicide protesting the conditions of an inhumane world."[1] Jones, whose ideology was a dangerous blend of Marxist liberation theology and his own personal megalomania, claimed that he was the prophetic reincarnation of Jesus, Buddha, Lenin, and Gandhi. The Jonestown mass suicide is the second largest mass civilian death in US history, surpassed only by the terrorist attacks of September 11, 2001. Those who died at Jonestown did not have a duty to die in the service of their faith; their religion was no better than a fraud. However, just as with suicides undertaken for a political cause, suicides for a religious cause are dubious to the extent that claims of religion are dubious. As much uncertainty as there is concerning the nature of justice, there is even greater uncertainty concerning the claims of the various religions. Religious diversity and disagreement are the norm in human civilization, with Christians, Muslims, Hindus, and many other religious groups each claiming that their God and their faith is the sole true one. Given the uncertainty of religious claims, we should be reluctant to conclude that suicides in the service of any religion do in fact advance truth. They are equally likely to be pointless and tragic deaths, like those of Jones's followers.

1   Jim Jones, "Transcript of Recovered FBI tape Q 42," The Jonestown Institute. 2001 (http://jonestown.sdsu.edu/AboutJonestown/Tapes/Tapes/DeathTape/Q042.html).

I am not suggesting that there is no such thing as justice, or that there is no true religion, although I am more skeptical about the former than the latter. I intend only to point out that an easy confidence in dying in the service of such causes is misplaced. There could well be a political or religious cause for which dying satisfies the Weightiness Principle. I am instead suggesting that suicides motivated by political or religious causes are required only if we are sufficiently confident in the justness or the truth of such causes—and that we have strong reasons to doubt, on any particular occasion, that in ending one's life for such a cause, there really is a basic moral duty that is fulfilled by suicide.

Doubts about suicides in the service of religious or political causes also flow from the Means Principle. Surely some of these suicides are the most effective way to advance a political or religious cause, yet suicide is hardly the only method of advancing a worthwhile cause and should probably be used only as a last resort. Some suicides may well succeed in advancing these causes to some degree, but might not more standard—and less dramatic—methods of advocacy be at least as effective as suicide? Determining the answers to such questions requires addressing complicated counterfactual questions. For instance, Đức's suicide was highly effective in drawing attention to the per-secution of Buddhists, but was it the most effective means? Could he have achieved his aims equally well with another dramatic gesture (a hunger strike or an act of civil disobedience)? After all, a good many causes have succeeded without their advocates engaging in suicide (for instance, the American civil rights movement, or the struggle against apartheid in South Africa).

Therefore, there are strong reasons to doubt that there is a duty to die in the service of a political or religious cause. The worries I have raised do not show this directly; rather, they ground a powerful presumption against a duty to die. There is, however, one kind of case in which it is more likely that a person has a duty to die for a political cause. That is when the person has explicitly promised to put his or her life at risk in the service of the state. Spies, govern-ment agents, and soldiers (at least when not drafted) take oaths in which they agree to subject themselves to personal risk in the course of fulfilling their occupational duties. In some cases, that oath demands suicide. A spy who is threatened with torture and reasonably believes that he will divulge state se-crets under torture could have a duty to die so as to prevent those secrets from being revealed. These are, however, exceptional cases, since they occur in those rare situations in which individuals have fully and unambiguously consented to the state's authority, thus providing the rationale for their having a duty to die in support of the state.

Suicide Ordered by the State

Another situation where it might seem plausible that a person has a duty to die is when his or her suicide is ordered by state authorities. The most famous example of this is undoubtedly the philosopher Socrates, who was convicted in ancient Athens of impiety and corrupting the youth. Though Socrates might have been able to avoid his punishment by going into exile, he was sentenced to drink a solution made with hemlock, a poisonous herb.

Do we have a duty to submit to a suicide order issued by political authorities? As with suicide for a political or religious cause, suicide at the behest of state authorities can be investigated only by exploring other, larger philosophical questions. The duty to submit to a suicide order is a binding duty only if there is a binding duty to do what the state commands. But is there such a duty in the first place? This is the question of political obligation. Most of us tend to take for granted that we have a moral duty to obey the laws and legal directives of the nations in which we live, but since the time of Plato, many philosophers have not taken such a duty for granted and have sought to provide justifications for political obligation. (Several of these justifications are described in Plato's dialogue *Crito*.) John Locke and Thomas Hobbes, for instance, claimed that we have a duty to obey the state because we have, in some fashion or other, consented to the authority of the state that issues and enforces the law. Other philosophers have maintained that we owe the state a debt of gratitude for having benefitted us, while others have argued that, as citizens, we are members of a group to whom we owe obligations, much as we owe obligations to our family. As with our earlier concern with political justice, political obligation is much too large a philosophical question to be tackled in a work devoted to the philosophical issues surrounding suicide. Suffice it to say, however, that all of the main justifications given for our having a duty to obey the state are problematic.

Take, for instance, the justification associated with Hobbes and Locke, appealing to consent. The claim underlying this justification is that we must obey the state because we have consented to its authority. What, exactly, counts as consenting? Is consenting a matter of verbal behavior, the way that new citizens take an oath of loyalty? If so, then only a handful of us have a duty to obey the state, since we became citizens more as a matter of luck than choice, based on where we were born or where our parents lived. Indeed, as many critics of the consent justification have noted, most of us have no opportunity to consent or not to the state's authority. Some advocates of the consent justification of political obligation respond that such objections construe the notion of consent too narrowly. Perhaps we consent to the state's authority implicitly, by paying taxes, voting, or receiving benefits from the state (driving on public roads, being educated in public schools). Yet it is not obvious how these actions result in a person's agreeing to the state's authority. Most of us pay our taxes because the state threatens to punish us if we do not, so paying taxes is the result of coercion rather than consent. Voting might be taken to imply consent to the state's authority, but again that is not entirely clear. Voting may be motivated by sheer self-interest rather than by any acceptance or endorsement of a state's authority. Furthermore, if voting implies consent to the state's authority, then presumably *not* voting implies that a person has not consented to a state's authority, which has the surprising consequence that many people in democratic societies do not recognize the state's authority. In addition, we may gladly receive the benefits that come from living in a political society, but critics of consent theory point out that simply receiving benefits is not the same as *accepting* those benefits or the authority of those who provide the benefits.

Consent theory is but one approach to political obligation, yet other accounts of political obligation have also been subject to strenuous critique. It is objections to consent theory (and to other justifications of political obligation) that have led some thinkers—those known as philosophical anarchists—to conclude that, whatever the merits of having political authority at all, there is *no* general duty to obey the state simply because it orders us to do so. Again, I can hardly hope to settle the philosophical debates concerning political obligation here. But without a powerful and relatively uncontroversial justification of political obligation, we are left with the anarchists' conclusion that we have no general duty to obey the state as such. If there is no such duty, then there is no duty to submit to a state's demand that we end our lives, and there is no duty to die stemming from state orders. In terms of our two principles, suicide ordered by the state is not likely to satisfy the Weightiness Principle. It would if there were a basic duty to obey the state's directives, but as I have argued here, it is far from clear that there is such a duty. Of course, a person ordered to end her life may opt for suicide if the alternative to suicide is state execution. This does not show that the suicide is morally obligatory, however.

Suicide to Unburden Others

In the 1990s, the philosopher John Hardwig published a series of articles arguing that individuals who, due to illness, physical decline, or similar reasons, become burdensome to their families and loved ones, can come to have a duty to die. Hardwig wrote in one of these articles:

> A serious illness in a family is a misfortune. It is usually nobody's fault; no one is responsible for it. But we face choices about how we will respond to this misfortune. That's where the responsibility comes in and fault can arise. Those of us with families and loved ones always have a duty not to make selfish or self-centered decisions about our lives. We have a responsibility to try to protect the lives of loved ones from serious threats or greatly impoverished quality, certainly an obligation not to make choices that will jeopardize or seriously compromise their futures. ... It is out of these responsibilities that a duty to die can develop.[1]

Interpreting Hardwig's argument can be tricky, but his line of thought appears to be this: a person can find herself in a situation where, by continuing to live, she is imposing burdens on her family or loved ones. These burdens may be financial—in many countries, such as the US, medical care for the extremely ill can bankrupt families, especially those that do not have health insurance—or they may be emotional or psychological, as when a family member needs round-the-clock attention. When these burdens become extreme, Hardwig argues, a person can have a duty to die if dying is the only way to relieve these unfair burdens. To insist on continuing to live, Hardwig says, is in effect to demand that others keep us alive regardless of the burdens our lives impose on other people. Again, Hardwig can be a tricky philosopher to interpret, but he takes this line of reasoning to support the conclusion that people may sometimes have a duty to initiate events that they intend will result in their deaths; that is to say, they have a duty to commit suicide.

---

1   "Is there a duty to die?," *Hastings Center Report* 27 (1997): 36.

Hardwig's argument captures an important moral insight: we are not free-floating individuals whose existence is cost free. At various times in the course of life, we exist thanks to the efforts or resources of others, most especially during childhood. Sometimes we become costly to others at later stages of life, and surely it is a mark of moral maturity to be mindful of the costs we impose on others. But Hardwig defends a more specific claim: that a morally mature individual would recognize that if the burdens she imposes are great enough, she has a duty to end her life. In this respect, Hardwig's position suggests an intriguing twist on the role responsibilities argument from Chapter Two: the original role responsibilities argument sought to argue that suicide was morally impermissible because it violated our duties to specific individuals to whom we have intimate ties, such as friends, loved ones, or family. Hardwig in effect argues that sometimes our role responsibilities *require* suicide.

Once again, we can analyze this argument for a duty of suicide by invoking the Weightiness and Means Principles. Let us assume, for the sake of argument, that in the cases Hardwig envisions, the Means Principle is typically satisfied: that dying is the most efficacious means to fulfilling the basic moral duty of not imposing excessive and unfair burdens on others. But even granting this, I have doubts that Hardwig's position satisfies the Weightiness Principle. To see why, it is interesting to observe that Hardwig also discusses the Captain Oates case and concludes that Oates had a duty to die. But there is an important moral distinction between the Oates case and the situations Hardwig has in mind, namely when people have lengthy illnesses or other conditions that render them dependent and burdensome. The distinction is this: if Oates had not exercised his duty to die, he probably would have put the lives of the other members of the expedition at risk. In contrast, those who burden others in Hardwig's sense put the economic or psychological well-being of others at risk, but they do not typically pose a risk to their lives. In concluding that Oates had a duty to die, Hardwig is in effect claiming that the burden Oates would have imposed by continuing to live—namely, risking his colleagues' lives—was great enough that he had a duty to die so as to relieve them of that burden. Put in terms of our Weightiness Principle, Hardwig thinks that the burdens Oates would have imposed on his colleagues by continuing to live are significantly greater than the harm that would have befallen him if he had continued. Here Hardwig is correct: putting many people's lives at risk is a significantly greater burden than the harm that an already ill, and possibly dying, Oates would suffer from death.

Of course, burdens vary in how burdensome they are. Some burdens are mild, and we should have no reservation whatsoever about expecting others to bear them on our behalf. The question that arises, then, is whether those who burden others in the ways Hardwig proposes (by being financially or emotionally burdensome) are burdensome *enough* to justify their having a duty to die and, in particular, whether the value of the burdens they impose is significantly greater than the harms they would suffer. Hardwig thinks so, but I am not fully convinced. When a person who, because of illness or other conditions, is burdensome to others, is she fulfilling a basic moral duty if she opts to die? Let us assume so for the sake of argument. But how shall we compare the value of what a burdensome person loses by dying with the burdens she imposes on others by living?

Death is a profound loss to a person who dies, and because of this we tend to see it as the greatest tragedy a person might suffer. The depth of the loss that accompanies death is why we might find it difficult to relate to suicide bombers or martyrs. What could possibly be worth dying for? The depth of this loss is also why we think of capital punishment as the most serious of criminal punishments and why capital criminals typically take every measure to avoid their executions, despite the fact that their likely fate should they succeed in avoiding execution—lifetime incarceration—itself involves staggering deprivations and losses. Perhaps we avoid death, and see it as the greatest evil we might suffer, because we misunderstand death or its nature. The Stoic philosophers thought so. But it is not obviously irrational to think of death as the worst possible tragedy a person can face: death is, for that individual, the end of the world. Their hopes and aspirations terminate, they are disconnected from all of their cares, and they no longer exert any influence on the world. There is a reason, then, why few of us would willingly trade death for almost any other good.

The losses or burdens that ill or dependent individuals impose on others can be severe as well, no doubt. As Hardwig notes, those responsible for caring for ill or dependent individuals may end up bankrupt, may end up damaging their own mental or physical well-being because of the stresses of providing such care, may have to postpone their careers, and may have to direct financial resources away from others to whom they are obligated (as when parents dip into the college savings designated for their children in order to pay for medical expenses for their aging parents). These are substantial burdens, not to be dismissed lightly, but they are not, in my estimation, significantly greater than the loss a burdensome person would suffer if she died. Indeed, if our intuitive judgment that death is a distinctive and unsurpassable loss is correct, then not only are these burdens not greater than the loss of death, but nor do they compare to the loss effected by death. Thus, Hardwig's attempt to justify a duty to die does not satisfy the Weightiness Principle and is therefore unsuccessful.

It is important to appreciate that my critique of Hardwig's position does not deny that some people burden others in profound ways. My critique only raises questions about whether these burdens are sufficient to satisfy the Weightiness Principle. Moreover, my critique takes seriously the notion that Hardwig intended to defend a *duty* to die, i.e., a requirement of suicide. Nothing in my critique suggests that those who are burdensome in the way Hardwig identifies may not be morally permitted to end their lives.

Suicide to Prevent the Deaths of Others

The final argument that we should consider is when a person's suicide might save the lives of others.

In the film *Star Trek II*, the crew of the space cruiser Enterprise is threatened by radioactivity emitted from the cruiser's engineering deck. Captain Spock, the ship's highly logical Vulcan first officer, chooses to enter the engineering deck and repair the damaged equipment, realizing that the radiation he will be exposed to will almost certainly kill him. Spock enters the deck, and as he undertakes the repairs his body slowly weakens. His work completed, Spock gives a moving explanation of his actions to his commander and friend, Admiral Kirk, saying, "the needs of the many outweigh the needs of the few."

Of course, the example of Mr. Spock is science fiction (though not so farfetched as we might imagine: workers at modern-day nuclear plants have sometimes been asked to expose themselves to strong doses of radiation in order to prevent the leakage of radiation that might harm or kill larger numbers of people). Before considering the implications of such an example for the duty to die, it is worth reminding ourselves that Spock's death would count as a suicide based on the criteria I defended in Chapter One. Death was not part of Spock's *intention*, since he did not enter the engineering deck with the aim of dying, nor was his death the means to his aim of saving the Enterprise crew. However, Spock's death was intentional, inasmuch as he foresaw the likelihood of his death and thereby endorsed his death as a side-effect of his chosen means. Hence, Spock offers a useful example of a suicidal act justified on the grounds that his death saved the lives of others.

My suspicion is that our reactions to such an example tend to fall into two categories. One reaction is that Spock's self-sacrifice is certainly morally permissible, even heroic, but not morally required. On this view, Spock deserves the hero's burial he in fact receives later in the film because he did more than he was morally obliged to do. Indeed, this fact—that he goes beyond the demands of duty—is what makes his actions heroic. The other reaction is that Spock has a duty to die because he has to prevent the deaths of the Enterprise crew. On this view, Spock does exactly what morality asks of him—no more, no less.

I come down closer to the side of the latter than the former. First, acting heroically is compatible with having a duty to die. It can sometimes be the case that what a person is morally obligated to do still requires courage and selflessness. An American Secret Service agent is morally obligated to put her life on the line to protect the President, even though doing so certainly requires courage and self-sacrifice that we understandably think of as heroic. Hence, it is coherent to say that Spock acts heroically in doing what he is obligated to do. Second, Spock's death satisfies the two principles we have been using in analyzing the duty to die. Given the imminence of threat to the crew members, Spock's entering the engineering deck and knowingly exposing himself to the lethal radiation are the most effective means of saving the ship and its crew. Thus, Spock's act satisfies our Means Principle. Does it also satisfy the Weightiness Principle—does his dying satisfy a basic moral duty whose moral significance is significantly greater than the risk or harm he suffers as a result? Spock dies, no doubt a substantial loss to himself and to others, but in doing so he saves hundreds of other innocent lives. Do we have a duty to save innocent lives when we can? This is arguable. Philosophical egoists may argue that our only duties are to ourselves and our own interests, but if we have any duties toward others, keeping them alive is perhaps the most central or basic of those duties. Furthermore, this duty increases in stringency the larger the number of persons whose lives are threatened. Now one might worry, in connection with the Weightiness Principle, just how "outnumbered" a person has to be in order for that principle to be satisfied and for there to be a duty to die. For instance, what if Spock would have saved ten lives by repairing the ship? Would he have had a duty to die then? What if it was just one person that he would save? Would that trigger a duty to die?

The short answer is that we should not deny that numbers *matter* in deter-mining whether a person has a duty to die in order to save other human lives. If I can save all of human civilization only by swallowing a capsule of arsenic, I am morally obligated to do so. But where is the line here—how many lives would my suicide have to save in order for me to have a duty to die? I make no pretense of proposing an exact number of lives that ground a duty to die in order that that number of lives may be saved. The ability to save two lives through one's own suicide establishes a stronger *presumption* in favor of hav-ing a duty to die than saving one other life, and so too does the ability to save three lives through one's own suicide establish a still stronger presumption, etc. Yet we do not necessarily need an exact criterion for the number of lives a person would save through his suicide in order to reach defensible conclusions about particular cases. A comparison: imagine reading a book whose first page is clearly blue, whose last page is clearly green, and each successive page is more green and less blue. There may well be disagreement about exactly which of the pages in the middle of the book are green or blue. Do the pages shift from blue to green after the fiftieth page? After the seventieth? After the hundredth? Note that although we may not be sure about the answer, such uncertainty casts no doubt on our belief that the first page is clearly blue and the last clearly green. Uncertainty about where a boundary lies should not lead us to second guess our judgments about examples that are clearly on one side of the boundary or the other. So too with the duty to die to save others: we may not be sure precisely how many lives need to be saved in order to trigger a duty to die, but this leaves our judgments about uncontroversial cases intact. The case of Dr. Spock, though fictional, is relatively uncontroversial, precisely because, as Spock says, the needs of *many* outweigh the needs of the *few*.

For a more down–to-earth example, consider again our Foxhole Jumper scenario from Chapter One, the soldier who leaps upon a live grenade in order to spare his comrades. Doubtless his sacrifice is morally admirable, but is it morally required? We can again apply the Weightiness and Means Principles to analyze this example. Our soldier in the Foxhole Jumper example is probably correct in thinking that the only action available to him to save his comrades is to jump upon the grenade, so it is plausible to think that the Means Principle is satisfied in this case. And the Weightiness Principle? Again, that will hinge on the number of lives Foxhole Jumper would save through his suicidal act, and as I argued above, we need not settle that question to conclude that there is *some* number of lives saved that would make it true that Foxhole Jumper has a duty to die. Some may think two lives is enough, while others will insist on many more. Again, our concern here is with whether the duty to prevent the deaths of others *can* justify a duty to die, and I contend that a reasonable case can be made for such a thesis.

Conclusion

On the whole, I am skeptical that there is anything more than a rarely instantiated duty to die. Of the kinds of cases we have considered—suicide in the service of a political or religious cause, suicide by order of the state, suicide to relieve burdens to others, and suicide to save the lives of others—only the last encompasses situations where the Weightiness and Means Principles are ever likely to be satisfied. Of course, this does not show that in the other cases suicide is impermissible—only that it is not required as a matter of moral duty.

Further Reading

Cosculluela (1995) investigates the possibility of a duty to die. Plato's dialogue *Crito* is the starting point for almost all philosophical discussions of political obligation. Hardwig (1997a) and (1997b) outline his defense of a duty to die, and his articles have inspired a great deal of discussion, much of which can be found in the anthology by Humber and Almeder (2000). I criticize Hardwig's position in Cholbi (2010). Hardwig offers replies to some of his earlier critics in his 2000 collection.

five

Suicide Prevention and Intervention

Suicide is a fundamental human right. This does not mean that it is morally desirable. It only means that society does not have the moral right to interfere.[1]

UP TO THIS POINT, the perspective taken on the ethics of suicide has been that of the suicidal individual: Chapters Two, Three, and Four addressed whether it is morally permissible or obligatory for a person to engage in suicide. However, this perspective is clearly too narrow, for suicide also raises ethical questions for people other than the one considering suicide. Specifically, what are our moral obligations to suicidal people, and do we ever have a duty to prevent others from taking their lives?

Here I will suggest that although many of the measures we can take to prevent or intervene in suicide are morally benign, some measures are problematic because they cause serious harm to suicidal individuals or because they interfere with those individuals' liberty or autonomy. After a discussion

---

1   Thomas Szasz, *The Untamed Tongue: A Dissenting Dictionary* (LaSalle, IL: Open Court, 1990), p. 250.

of the kinds of reasons that favor preventing or intervening in others' suicidal behavior, I will suggest that the fact that suicide is often irrational and distinctive in its harms gives us a powerful reason for such intervention or prevention, despite objections that such acts would be paternalistic.

Benign vs. Problematic Measures

To begin, not all measures we might use to prevent or intervene in suicide are morally problematic. There are a good many measures that are likely to reduce the number of suicides without raising moral "red flags" at all, including the following:

- public education campaigns advertising suicide prevention resources;
- better training of doctors, educators, and others to recognize the signs of suicidal thinking;
- wider access to health care in general;
- the creation of suicide hotlines or "walk-in" resources;
- support for suicide-related research.

In saying these measures are morally benign, I mean only that they do not seem to have a negative effect on people. No obligations owed to specific individuals are violated through public education campaigns, for example. This does not mean that such measures raise no difficulties at all; they are not necessarily easy to implement, and many of them would require public funds to support them. Being morally unproblematic does not, therefore, make these measures *politically* unproblematic.

There are two reasons to think that such measures are benign from a moral perspective, however. First, none of the measures listed is harmful to individuals. They do not cause physical injury, mental anguish, or the like. Second, none of these measures interferes with individuals' liberty or autonomy. Merely being exposed to information about suicide or having available medical or counseling resources for those considering suicide does not compel anyone to do anything they would otherwise be unwilling to do.

Conversely, when a prevention or intervention measure is harmful or interferes with liberty or autonomy, this *does* present reasons for moral concern. Indeed, we should, all things being equal, be more reluctant to employ a measure the more it possesses one or both of these features. Hence, the following measures are, to varying degrees, morally problematic because they have at least one of the two features described above:

- compulsory medical and psychological treatment for mental disorders associated with suicidal behavior;
- incarceration, institutionalization in hospitals, or other forms of physical restraint;
- requiring suicidal individuals to use antidepressants or other medications;
- subjecting suicidal individuals to brain surgery or other bodily interventions;
- the use of deception, misinformation, or any similar means to secure the suicidal individual's consent to any of the aforementioned measures on this list.

Again, these measures share morally problematic features, features that demand a moral justification be provided in order for them to be used.

Why Prevent or Intervene?

Before considering whether more problematic forms of prevention or intervention could be morally justified, we must first consider a basic question: what moral reasons are there for preventing or intervening in others' suicidal behavior in the first place?

First, that suicide is morally impermissible is one seemingly powerful reason for prevention or intervention. If a person intends to do something that is morally wrong, then it would appear to be morally obligatory for us to prevent it if we can. We have an obligation, it would seem, to prevent others from engaging in wanton violence and killing. So if suicide is morally wrong, then presumably stopping suicide is morally right.

As a basis for preventing or intervening in others' suicidal behavior, this appeal to the immorality of suicide is limited in two ways. First, we observed in Chapter Two that there is no generally sound argument for the moral impermissibility of suicide. There may be particular suicidal acts that are impermissible, but we cannot establish a *comprehensive* right to intervene in or prevent suicide on the basis of suicide being morally wrong.

Second, as we observed in Chapter Three, even when suicide is morally wrong, it does not follow directly from this premise that compelling a suicidal person to live is morally permissible. For the mere fact that another person fails to fulfill a moral obligation does not entail that we may act so as to get them to fulfill that obligation. Again, exactitude in this area is unlikely, but whether such interference in another person's behavior is permissible hinges most centrally on whether the interference itself violates a moral obligation, the stringency of that obligation, and the importance of the moral wrong being prevented. The more serious or wide ranging the interference, the more serious must the moral wrong be that we seek to prevent. If I can stop a car thief by shouting "get away from that car!", then I morally ought to do so: I violate no moral obligation at all by shouting at him. But it is nevertheless possible to go morally overboard here: if I pull out a revolver and shoot the would-be car thief, I do prevent the theft but only by means of a moral wrong no less serious than the theft itself. So if suicide is morally wrong, how serious a wrong is it? As I have noted, for some philosophers, including Augustine and supporters of the sanctity of life argument, suicide (because it is the willful taking of a human life) is no less a wrong than murder itself.

However, note that even among those who believe that suicide is morally wrong, opinions are likely to vary as to how serious a wrong it is, and many of the arguments for its impermissibility suggest that it is not as serious a wrong as murder. For proponents of the natural law argument, suicide might belong in the same moral category as other "corrupting" behaviors such as masturbation. Adherents of the property argument analogize suicide to theft, whereas the gift argument indicates that suicide is comparable to ingratitude. The variability in how these arguments categorize the morality of suicide suggests that, regardless of whether a credible case can be made for suicide being morally wrong, it is controversial just how serious a wrong it is in any case. But appealing to the moral wrongfulness of suicide in order to make a general case for intervention and prevention is more plausible if suicide is a very serious moral wrong. Indeed, using some of the coercive or harmful measures listed in the previous section requires that suicide be a very serious moral wrong. However, that cannot be easily assumed.

For these reasons, I am somewhat reluctant to rest the case for suicide intervention and prevention on the alleged immorality of the act. Suicide is often not immoral (except in exceptional cases), and even if it is immoral, serious disagreement exists about how serious a wrong it is. But there is another category of reasons to which we might appeal in order to justify prevention and intervention: that such behavior is the product of irrational thinking or is contrary to the suicidal person's interests. As we concluded in Chapter Three, many (if not most) suicides are irrational, being either the result of impaired cognition or contrary to the individual's interest. The apparent irrationality of much suicidal behavior provides us with a moral rationale for intervention because it is at least sometimes morally permissible for us to try to prevent people from behaving irrationally against their interests. Many motorcycle riders would not wear helmets if there were not laws requiring them to do so, and while there is doubtless a special pleasure that comes from traveling the open road with the wind whipping through one's hair, this does not seem worth the greatly increased risk of injury or death that riding helmetless brings.

Indeed, appealing to the irrationality of suicidal behavior provides a stronger rationale for suicide intervention and prevention efforts than appealing to its immorality. There is hardly any agreement about the moral permissibility of suicide, but an even-handed reading of the evidence concerning suicidal behavior suggests that much is, in various ways and to varying degrees, irrational. Of course, this conclusion should not be exaggerated, and many of the same qualifications that applied to justifying intervention or prevention on moral grounds apply here: how irrational the person's suicide would be, whether the means of intervention and prevention violate other moral obligations, how serious these obligations are—these are all factors that must be taken into account in determining the moral permissibility of intervening in or acting to prevent a suicidal act.

The Paternalism Objection

To some, my suggestion that preventing or intervening in suicidal behavior is morally permissible, at least on the grounds that much of that behavior is irrational, is itself morally suspect. They may invoke the authority of John Stuart Mill and his well-known Harm Principle:

> The object of this Essay is to assert one very simple principle, as entitled to govern absolutely the dealings of society with the individual in the way of compulsion and control, whether the means used be physical

force in the form of legal penalties, or the moral coercion of public opinion. That principle is, that the sole end for which mankind are warranted, individually or collectively, in interfering with the liberty of action of any of their number, is self-protection. That the only purpose for which power can be rightfully exercised over any member of a civilized community, against his will, is to prevent harm to others. His own good, either physical or moral, is not sufficient warrant. He cannot rightfully be compelled to do or forbear because it will be better for him to do so, because it will make him happier, because, in the opinion of others, to do so would be wise, or even right.... The only part of the conduct of anyone, for which he is amenable to society, is that which concerns others. In the part which merely concerns himself, his independence is, of right, absolute. Over himself, over his own body and mind, the individual is sovereign.[1]

Mill forcefully articulates a very important moral ideal: that of opposition to paternalism. It is one thing, Mill argues, for us, acting individually or collectively as a society, to compel a person not to behave in ways that harm others. Indeed, preventing people from harming one another is the cornerstone of much of our legal, political, and moral apparatus. Few people would, for instance, not want the law to punish murder, theft, and physical assault, for such laws protect us against the worst sorts of harms others may do to us. But Mill argues that we have no right to compel people not to do what harms only themselves. Over our own bodies and minds, we are "sovereign," Mill asserts, and while individuals or a society may restrict a person's liberty in order to protect themselves, restricting or interfering with a person's liberty for his own good is not morally justified.

On its face, to advocate suicide intervention or prevention, as I have, violates Mill's Harm Principle. It appears to treat people, not as independent individuals capable of making up their own minds about what is best for themselves, but as children in need of protection against their own instincts. That, critics argue, is the very essence of paternalism.

But matters are not as simple as this. First, note that the Harm Principle tells us that interference with a person's behavior *solely* for their own good is unjustified. Yet many suicides *are* harmful to others: parents' suicides are often

---

1   *On Liberty and Other Writings* (Cambridge: Cambridge University Press, 1989), chapter 1.

harmful to their children, and many people are saddened when suicide occurs because they have suffered the loss of a loved one. This provides an additional reason to think that suicide prevention or intervention is morally permissible: suicide is often an act that "concerns others," as Mill might have put it. In those cases, the Harm Principle simply does not apply.

Second, the Harm Principle tells us that we cannot interfere with others' liberty for their own good. But as I noted above, many anti-suicide measures are morally unproblematic because they do not interfere with a person's liberty. Education campaigns, improved medical education, the creation of suicide hotlines, and so on do not interfere with anyone's liberty. Admittedly, the Harm Principle should give us further pause concerning the more coercive or harmful anti-suicide measures discussed above, but it does not show that all anti-suicide measures are morally impermissible.

Yet critics may still worry that I have not dealt with the heart of their complaint: that many of the ways by which we might prevent or intervene in suicidal behavior are wrong because they amount to paternalistic interference with individuals' right to decide for themselves what happens to their bodies. Granted, to argue that we should intervene in or prevent suicide because many suicides are irrational is to argue that we ought to interfere with their liberty, but the central question is whether this would amount to *wrongful* interference with their liberty.

To appreciate why suicide intervention and prevention efforts do not necessarily wrongfully interfere with liberty, consider again a phenomenon discussed in Chapter Three: child suicide. I do not believe that any reasonable person could hold that efforts to prevent or intervene in the suicides of children are morally unjustified. Again, this need not entail taking every possible measure to prevent minors from ending their lives, but surely aggressive anti-suicide measures are appropriate in this area. Why are efforts to prevent childhood suicide not instances of objectionable paternalism? It is tempting to say that paternalism is wrong because it treats people as children, but children are, well, children. I would suggest a more substantive reason, however: childhood suicides are almost always irrational. Children are not likely to meet the cognitive and interest conditions outlined before: they often have unrealistic worldviews, are poor judges of their own long-term interests, act recklessly, and so on. Indeed, Mill himself recognized this fact and so he explicitly exempted children from the scope of the protections afforded by his Harm Principle.

However, children are not simply a benign counterexample for those who press this anti-paternalist objection. If the reason that children are not treated paternalistically when we act to prevent their suicides is that their suicides are irrational, then presumably it would not be wrongfully paternalistic to act to prevent the suicides of *adults* whose suicides are irrational either. At the very least, it is hard to see why the chronological age of a suicidal person should matter to how we may respond to her suicidal intentions. And as I argued in Chapter Three, many, if not most, suicidal acts exhibit some species of irrationality, often due to the distorting effects of mental illness. That it may be permissible to interfere with a person's behavior when that behavior stems from irrationality is a thesis that Mill, despite the strong anti-paternalistic language with which he presents his Harm Principle, would endorse. He allows, for instance, that it can be justifiable to interfere with a person's liberty if his actions rest on errors of fact. Mill gives the example of a person who is about to walk (unknowingly) across a rickety, damaged bridge. He concludes that it would be morally permissible to stop such a person from walking across the bridge in order to ascertain if he knows how dangerous it is. Mill thus tacitly acknowledges that the value of protecting a person's liberty from interference by others hinges on whether that liberty is being rationally exercised and, in particular, whether the person is adequately informed about the decision at hand.

My claim that the irrationality of suicide justifies attempting to prevent or intervene in suicidal behavior does not imply that we should intervene anytime a person intends to act irrationally. Practically speaking, that would be impossible, since people are frequently irrational. What seems to warrant suicide intervention and prevention efforts is not only that suicide is frequently irrational, but also that its harms are usually immediate, costly, and irreversible. Compare irrational suicide to another common instance of human irrationality: overeating. Gluttony is a common human vice, and many societies take measures to encourage healthy eating. Admittedly, overeating is often irrational, since it has long-term harms such as premature death, obesity, and other diseases. But these harms are importantly different from the harms of suicide. For one, the harms of suicide are immediate: a person who commits suicide is immediately deprived of all of the goods she may have enjoyed by continuing to live. The serious harms of overeating, on the other hand, generally develop over a lifetime: a person slowly becomes less mobile over time, develops diabetes or other diseases, and so on. But because the harms of overeating emerge gradually, we have less reason to prevent or aggressively intervene in individuals' overeating. Not only do we have more opportunities to help people stop overeating, but they also have more opportunities to educate themselves, develop more self-control, and so on.

Second, many suicides are clearly very costly. An 18-year old college freshman who ends his life because of a difficult romantic breakup deprives the world of his future professional and personal accomplishments. Moreover, he deprives *himself* of whatever goods his future may hold, which (given his youth) are likely to be considerable. Overeating is harmful, but its costs are typically not as great. Discomfort and disease are often unpleasant, and shortened lifespans are regrettable, but the best estimates are that obesity reduces one's normal lifespan by less than one year on average. All in all, then, suicide's harms are almost always far greater.

Finally, suicide and its harms are distinctive in their irreversibility. A person who overeats often can reverse the harms of overeating through changes in behavior, medical treatments, and so on. But suicide is final: once done, its harms cannot be undone. The harms of suicide thus possess distinctive features that many other self-inflicted harms do not: features that warrant efforts to stop suicide.

Recall Mill's remark that a person may not "rightfully be compelled to do or forbear because it will be better for him to do so, because it will make him happier, because, in the opinion of others, to do so would be wise, or even right...." But we may then ask: What if the person would hold a different opinion about his actions, and would not even perform them, were he sufficiently rational? Such is often the case with suicide, I have argued. Were an individual sufficiently rational in thinking about the facts and circumstances surrounding her decision of whether to end her life, she often would choose not to do so. And it is not obviously wrong or objectionably paternalistic to compel a person not to end her life if she would opt not to end her life were she sufficiently rational.

Morally Permissible Anti-suicide Measures

Anti-suicide measures motivated by the goal of stopping a person from doing what her more rational self would recognize as irrational are not necessarily wrongfully paternalistic. Again, this does not imply that we are morally permitted to do just *anything* to a person contemplating suicide when that suicide is irrational, so we should now reconsider the morality of various specific anti-suicide measures, especially those we classified earlier as morally suspect rather than benign.

One conclusion to be drawn from our discussion so far is that measures taken to prevent or intervene in others' suicidal behavior are more morally justified to the extent that, first, they do not cause the individual harm, and second, they do not wrongfully or paternalistically interfere with a person's liberty. We should therefore return to those anti-suicide measures that are most morally troubling because they are harmful or interfere with individual liberty or autonomy. I mentioned earlier that these include compulsory medical and psychological treatment for mental disorders associated with suicidal behavior; incarceration, institutionalization in hospitals, or other forms of physical restraint; requiring suicidal individuals to use antidepressants or other medications; subjecting suicidal individuals to brain surgery or other bodily interventions; and the use of deception or misinformation to secure the suicidal individual's consent to any of these other measures.

Of these measures, the most morally worrisome are surgical interventions. In the mid-twentieth century, it was not uncommon for mentally ill patients in institutions to undergo lobotomies, surgical procedures in which all nervous system connections to and from the brain's prefrontal cortex are severed. The procedure itself is grisly: in what came to be known as "ice-pick lobotomy," a patient was put under local anesthesia, then an ice pick was placed just above an individual's eye socket, hammered into his brain, and then wiggled around in order to sever the nerve connections in the prefrontal cortex. Clinically speaking, lobotomies were somewhat effective as a suicide prevention measure. Nowadays, however, they are considered one of the moral horror stories of modern medicine, because they "worked" by introducing a wide range of mental disabilities and personality changes, including a kind of reduced, almost catatonic, sense of emotion and motivation. Of course, lobotomies are a dramatically invasive form of psychosurgery, and many forms of psychosurgery in use today are far less invasive and have fewer long-term effects. But psychosurgery permanently modifies a person's body, and more specifically the brain, the very seat of a person's consciousness and personality; thus, surgical interventions are direct assaults on a person's identity and autonomy. Furthermore, many surgical interventions carry significant medical risk and deprive individuals of crucial elements of their mental life (for example, psychosurgery can reduce a person's susceptibility to pleasure).

Forcing suicidal individuals to take drugs that suppress suicidal thinking is nearly as morally worrisome as surgical interventions. Like surgical interventions, drugs modify a person's patterns of thinking and feeling and are therefore direct interventions into her autonomy. Many drugs prescribed to diminish suicidal behavior not only have significant side-effects, but may well have long-term effects that go unrecognized. Many critics have noted that drugs are often approved for patient use without long-term studies of their effects. Taken together, these facts about drugs suggest that compelling patients to take medications, like surgical interventions, threaten individual autonomy and can cause lasting harm, making their forced use highly suspect as methods of suicide intervention or prevention.

Placing suicidal individuals in institutions, monitoring them, or physically restraining them in order to prevent suicidal behavior—these are also morally troubling, but, I would suggest, less so than either surgical interventions or forced drugging. Certainly, these measures can involve significant invasions of personal privacy and limitations on physical mobility and so should worry us for those reasons alone. However, they infringe on individuals' autonomy in a more limited way than do surgical interventions or forced drugging: they do so in a physical sense, either actually preventing movement or by permitting others to observe one's movement and behavior. In contrast, forced drugging or surgical interventions more profoundly modify a person's will because they influence thinking, reasoning, and feeling. Surgical or pharmaceutical interventions limit one's consciousness, whereas incarceration, surveillance, and restraint limit how conscious thought can be acted upon. On top of that, while the latter measures are harmful, their harms do not appear to be as lasting or as permanent. Although the conditions at many mental hospitals and other treatment facilities could be much improved, in most cases they have still improved substantially since the apex of institutionalization in the 1950s.

What of other forms of compulsory treatment, such as psychotherapy or counseling? Conventional "talk therapy" poses few moral problems as a measure to prevent or intervene in suicidal plans. Admittedly, such therapy is time-consuming, inconvenient, and often slow in its progress, but nothing compels patients to cooperate in therapy, and even when they do cooperate, the therapy is generally not harmful and does not interfere significantly with their liberty. Even those who are not cured by therapy often acknowledge that it stems suicidal thinking and leads to gains in self-understanding and perspective. Psychotherapy also tends to increase patients' compliance with other forms of treatment, such as medication.

Among other forms of treatment for suicidal thought, electroconvulsive therapy (ECT) is probably the most controversial. Used almost exclusively on patients whose depression does not respond to other treatments and drugs, ECT involves causing seizure-level electrical stimulation in the brain through a pair of electrodes. There is strong evidence that such electrical stimulation is an effective measure against depression, mania, and suicidal thinking, especially when it is followed by other forms of treatment. Thousands of people throughout the world have received ECT, and in most cases their experiences are largely positive. However, serious worries exist about the effects of ECT on long-term memory and cognition. Critics also complain that ECT is often administered without patients' informed consent by medical professionals with little training and little understanding of the legal and ethical requirements to which ECT is subject. And although critics rarely say so, I suspect that one reason for their opposition to the use of ECT is that it offers the very unsettling spectacle of an anesthetized individual strapped to a hospital bed experiencing an artificial seizure; such a scene evokes pity and anger in observers. Even so, there do not seem to be strong, categorical arguments against the use of ECT as a measure to diminish suicidal thoughts, and it is surprisingly effective, especially for individuals for whom drug treatment has not worked. In terms of our two criteria for evaluating anti-suicide measures—infringements on liberty or autonomy and the risk of harm—ECT is not completely benign, however. In the past, individuals deemed incompetent were sometimes subject to ECT against their wills, a powerful violation of their personal liberty. Concerns about the impact of ECT on cognition and memory should be taken seriously, but rather than these concerns constituting an argument against its use altogether, they strike me as an argument for the use of ECT under precisely the same conditions in which we would administer any other medical treatment: only under the supervision of trained medical professionals cognizant of the risks, and only to patients who give informed consent to the procedure.

Finally, desperation sometimes leads people to deceive individuals in order to prevent them from killing themselves. Deception is a central category of moral wrongs, and so the use of deception, even with the good intention of trying to help a suicidal person, is morally troubling. Furthermore, how wrong the use of deception is in such circumstances depends on what the individual is deceived into doing, and in general, the more serious the risk of harm or infringement on liberty, the more morally objectionable it is to deceive. So, based on the arguments I have made in this section, it is more objectionable to deceive a suicidal person in order to arrange for a surgical intervention than it is to deceive in order to get her to take antidepressants, for example.

One wrinkle here relates to a now familiar problem, namely irrationality or incompetence. To deceive a person is wrong because deception disables that person's ability to make decisions that reflect his own rational judgment. If I lie to another person (and my lie is believed), the result is that the other person may end up reaching judgments and making choices based on false beliefs, and in so doing end up thwarting her own ends. Indeed, that is often the very purpose of a lie—to move people to act in ways we want them to act, but contrary to their own aims or objectives. The perplexity that arises with using deception in order to prevent suicide is that many suicidal individuals are already subject to various forms of irrationality; that is, they are already prone to thinking and acting in ways that are contrary to their considered aims or objectives. This fact might tempt us to conclude that deceiving the suicidally irrational is not wrong at all: it cannot be wrong to deceive someone and thereby undermine their rationality if that person is already irrational, some might argue.

However, I do not accept that the irrationality or incompetence that suicidal individuals sometimes exhibit means that deceiving them is morally unproblematic. For one thing, rationality and competence come in degrees, and while it is fair to say that many suicidal individuals are *compromised* with respect to their rationality or competence, it does not follow that they are fully irrational or incompetent. Even in the deepest throes of suicidal thinking, many individuals can still be rationally engaged, deliberative, and reflective to some degree. Second, we should resist the conclusion that there is nothing problematic about deceiving those who are less than fully competent. Regardless of whether deceiving them does not have its typical or intended effect, the mere fact that we are attempting to deceive means that we are expressing a disregard for them as human agents. Moreover, that a suicidal individual is not fully competent or rational does not mean that deception does not interfere with her ability to deliberate or to formulate beliefs. Consider this example: suppose someone has long accepted some elaborate conspiracy theory—that the American military was responsible for the September 11 terrorist attacks, for instance. She is then presented with evidence demonstrating the implausibility of the theory but persists in believing it anyway.

With respect to explanation of the terrorist attacks, she is irrational. Would it then be permissible for others to lie to her by affirming her belief in the conspiracy ("yes, of course, 9/11 was an inside job")? Deceiving her is not obviously morally problem-free. Even though her belief formation processes are clearly not operating rationally, a lie nevertheless fails to respect her *capacity* for rational thought, even if this capacity is not in evidence in this particular instance. The way in which deception is wrong is not simply that it actually fails to respect a person's existing rationality. Rather, it fails to respect our capacity for rationality, and so a lie is not rendered innocuous because it is told to an irrational or less than fully competent person. The same is true, then, of deceiving the suicidally irrational. Deceiving them can be wrong even if they are less than fully rational or competent because doing so disrespects their rational capacity. Thus, irrationality or incompetence does not provide carte blanche to deceive suicidal individuals.

My aim here is not to show which of the morally worrisome anti-suicide measures are morally permissible and which are not. Rather, by ranking these measures, I mean only to suggest that the use of any such measure must be weighed against the seriousness of the threat of suicide. In other words, the more morally dubious an intervention or prevention measure, the more probable it must be that the person in question would end her life in the absence of such a measure. Anti-suicide measures should therefore be used *proportionally* to the seriousness of the suicidal intentions or plans they aim to prevent. This entails that even the most morally worrisome measures may be used when a profoundly irrational individual is wholly determined to end her life. Again, I offer no exact guidelines for when various anti-suicide measures should be used, but the proportionality standard at least offers a framework for rationally investigating the question.

The proportionality standard becomes more useful when our assessments of an individual's risk for suicide are more accurate, and as any clinician can attest, this is a complicated, but not utterly hopeless, business. The most direct evidence of suicide risk is obviously a person's own behavior and statements, including life-threatening acts and statements of intent to engage in suicide. Indeed, the most powerful predictor that a person is likely to be suicidal in the future is her having made a suicide attempt in the past. However, a careful clinician will also take into account the presence of anxiety, emotional turbulence, or feelings of hopelessness; past diagnoses of mental disorder; drug or alcohol abuse; access to lethal means, such as weapons or prescription drugs;

access to medical or psychological care; sources of stress; and social isolation and social support, among other factors. Here psychiatry becomes as much an art as a science, requiring judgments that, because they must incorporate all these factors, are likely to be imperfect even if generally reliable.

Finally, we ought not to forget that multiple or sequential anti-suicide measures are often the best course of action. Many suicidal individuals are best served by a course of treatment including hospitalization and drug therapy, with each of these elements being removed from the patient's treatment protocol as his condition improves. A large number of studies support the conclusion that a combination of drugs and psychotherapy is more effective in treating depression and the other mental illnesses associated with suicide than are either drugs or psychotherapy alone.

Paternalism, autonomy, and Ulysses directives

As I have noted, one potential barrier to suicide intervention or prevention is that some anti-suicide measures threaten the autonomy of suicidal individuals. However, there is one device that would appear to reduce this threat.

In recent decades, advance directives—legal documents, also known as living wills, that lay out how a person desires that others should respond in future medical emergencies —have become very common. Typically, an advance directive indicates the treatments that an individual wishes to receive or forego if she becomes unable to make on-the-spot decisions about her treatment in a subsequent medical emergency. For example, an advance directive will often state whether a person who becomes unable to choose her own course of treatment wishes to receive dialysis, be placed on artificial respiration or nutrition, or be resuscitated in case of heart failure. A properly drafted advance directive is legally binding, meaning that family members and medical personnel are legally compelled to honor its content.

In recent decades, an analogous device has arisen for those who know they are prone to suicidal thinking. In what is known as a "Ulysses contract," a person indicates the measures she wishes to be undertaken on her behalf should she later need treatment for the symptoms of mental illness. These contracts get their name from the famous story of the Greek king Odysseus, whom the Romans later named Ulysses. Ulysses sought to hear the seductive song of the Sirens, but he feared it would drive him so mad he would be lured irreversibly into their clutches. Knowing that hearing the song would result in irrational but irresistible temptations, Ulysses had his crew tie him up to his ship's mast, under order that they not untie him even if he pleaded to be let loose. A modern-day Ulysses contract serves the same function: a person aware that she is at risk of making poor decisions due to the influence of mental illness can fashion a Ulysses contract describing whether she wishes to be medicated or institutionalized, for example. And, since suicidal thought is often associated with mental illness, Ulysses contracts may contain specific provisions addressing what is to be done when a person exhibits suicidal thoughts or behavior. Some of these contracts contain "no-suicide" clauses wherein an individual enters into an agreement with her therapist not to commit suicide. So imagine that a person with bipolar disorder experiences episodes of suicidal thinking during the depressive phases of her condition. She may, in consultation with her psychiatrist and family, draft a Ulysses contract specifying the measures to be taken during future episodes of such thinking. This contract could outline whether she should be medicated or institutionalized, what sort of supervision she would be subject to, and so on. Just as in the case of an ordinary medical advance directive, the expectation is that the individual's subsequent wishes will be respected by others.

It should be clear why Ulysses contracts are important with respect to the autonomy of suicidal individuals. Serious worries exist about the apparently paternalistic character of efforts to stop suicide, as we have seen, and some anti-suicide measures appear to wrongfully infringe on suicidal individuals' autonomy. However, such measures would be acceptable if they were permissible provisions of Ulysses contracts. In other words, if a person with a history of suicidal thought drafts a Ulysses contract that, say, permits him to be institutionalized during a later episode of suicidal thinking—even if during that later episode he expresses a desire not to be institutionalized—then it is not objectionably paternalistic to institutionalize him at that time. In doing so, we are not acting against his considered, rational wishes (assuming he was sufficiently rational at the time the contract was written), even though we are acting against his stated present wishes. And, as I argued earlier, what primarily matters in determining whether an anti-suicide measure is objectionably paternalistic is not whether it interferes with a person's behavior but whether it interferes with behavior that results from rational judgment and decision. Thus, in enforcing a Ulysses contract in an effort to prevent suicidal acts, we avoid the paternalism objection, for the resulting actions are authorized by the individual herself, as a form of pre-emptive or preventive consent against her recognized tendency to succumb to irrational patterns of thought and decision.

On the whole, then, many thorny moral problems concerning how we treat suicidal individuals could be lessened, if not resolved outright, if more such individuals entered into Ulysses contracts. Even the measures that we deemed highly morally problematic (compulsory medication, institutionalization, and the like) become far less problematic if the individual rationally consents to such measures, and with a Ulysses contract, a person rationally consents to such measures but in advance of when those measures will be needed to prevent her suicidal act. Few suicidal individuals enter into Ulysses contracts, however, mainly because few of them know about such possibilities.

That being said, several worries and limitations about Ulysses contracts deserve acknowledgment. First, it is morally permissible for others to apply the clauses of a Ulysses contract for an individual who entered into the contract while rationally competent but who has become incompetent. In doing so, we are assisting the person in realizing her rationally chosen interests. Some have argued, though, that we may apply the clauses of Ulysses contracts (and other advance directives) even when the person remains competent. But this view raises a puzzle: if a person is competent *now* to determine how she wishes others to respond to her suicidal tendencies, then why should we not honor her current competent wishes, even if those wishes contradict those of her earlier competent self? I myself am not convinced that Ulysses contracts should be honored when a competent individual states that she wishes to override her earlier contract. Such cases, where a competent individual seeks to have her earlier competent wishes overturned, are likely to be rare with respect to Ulysses directives that address suicidal behavior, for as I argued in Chapter Three, there are good reasons to think that suicidal thinking often renders individuals insufficiently rational to make decisions that reflect their interests. Therefore, the instances where an individual is both engaged in suicidal thinking but also rationally competent are likely to be few. Still, even in those rare instances, there is no obvious reason to honor the earlier competently drafted Ulysses contract rather than an individual's later competent choices. The competent individual who rejects the terms of her earlier Ulysses contract has done nothing more than change her mind, and while it can be understandable to be puzzled over such changes of mind, we do not hold people to their earlier rational decisions if later they rationally reject those earlier decisions. In this sense, talk of a Ulysses "contract" may be misleading.

Ordinarily, a person who enters into a contract cannot simply back out of it later on because she has changed her mind concerning how desirable it would be for the contract to be honored. But in the case of a Ulysses contract, two of the "parties" to the contract—i.e., the earlier self who drew it up and the later self to whom it is applied—are the same person, and so it is unclear why a person who, while deliberating rationally and competently, opts out of her earlier contract ought not to be treated in accordance with her later wishes. Respecting a person's autonomy means respecting her rational choices, so to disregard subsequent rational choices because they are at odds with earlier rational choices is to disrespect rather than honor a person's autonomy. Still, Ulysses contracts are designed specifically for situations in which a suicidal individual is *not* rationally competent, so this situation will arise only rarely. But my arguments suggest that Ulysses contracts should not be enforced for those who have suicidal thoughts while competent. Their later competent wishes supersede their earlier competent ones.

Hence, Ulysses contracts should be honored only when a suicidal individual who was competent at the time the contract was created becomes incompetent during an episode of suicidal thinking. But here is a second worry sometimes raised about Ulysses contracts. In fashioning such a directive, a person is making judgments about what is best for her during a future situation. We are interested in particular in her judgments concerning what should be done in episodes of suicidal thinking. But we might wonder whether a person really knows enough about those episodes—how she will think, feel, etc.—to plan for them. Compare the situation with medical advance directives. Suppose someone creates an advance directive in which he indicates that he would not wish to continue living if an injury resulted in permanent paralysis. Such a provision is understandable, since most people place strong value on physical mobility. Yet we might wonder whether a person can have sufficient understanding of what it might be to live life as a paralytic to be warranted in believing that such a life is not worth it. (Recall our earlier discussion from Chapter Three about our capacity to "appreciate" death.) If it really is not possible for a person to appreciate life as a paralytic, then perhaps we should not honor advance directives that depend on their knowing what they apparently do not know. Similarly, a person may not fully appreciate the depth of the despair associated with much suicidal thinking. If so, then shouldn't we disregard a person's Ulysses contract on the grounds that, however competent they are on the whole, they simply lack the evidence to make decisions about how they ought to be treated when such despair strikes?

In a word, no. We should not disregard a Ulysses contract outright on such grounds. For one thing, most Ulysses contracts are drafted *after* a person has been diagnosed with a mental illness and/or subsequent to an individual having an episode of suicidal thinking. Therefore, there are good reasons to think that the situation raised by this worry—where a person is making treatment decisions about a condition with which they are not familiar—will be uncommon. In most cases, then, a suicidal person will be sufficiently familiar with suicidal thinking and planning to know how she would want others to respond in the future. Moreover, the standard implied by these worries—that a person is competent to determine how others should treat them in a given set of circumstances only if the person has actually experienced that set of circumstances—is clearly unreasonable. For example, many medical advance directives state what a patient would like to occur if she falls into an irreversible coma. But note how ridiculous it would be to insist that her wishes should only be honored if she had actually had first-hand experience of being in an irreversible coma! The fact is that we often have to make choices based on less than complete knowledge or information. We do not know how we will feel if the car we are considering buying breaks down in a snowstorm, yet it does not seem unreasonable for us to decide whether to buy it even without such knowledge. We do not know what it is like to be married to the same person for two decades, yet it does not seem unreasonable to allow us to decide whether that is what we want. Typically, then, it is not reasonable to undermine or interfere with a person's choices concerning a future state of affairs simply because he lacks first-hand acquaintance with such states of affairs. Hence, not to honor a Ulysses directive because an otherwise competent individual lacks first-hand awareness of, say, having serious suicidal thoughts is unjustified. This does not obviate the need to consider whether a person having suicidal thoughts really is competent. If so, as I have argued, then we are obligated to honor the judgments made in the later suicidal state.

Though they are not unproblematic, Ulysses directives thus have the potential to answer many of the serious moral objections leveled at suicide prevention or intervention measures. In honoring a Ulysses directive, we honor a competent person's autonomy and do not treat her in ways that are objectionably paternalistic. This fact can render otherwise problematic anti-suicide measures morally permissible.

Availability of Lethal Means

One of the most vexing questions concerning suicide prevention is whether restricting access to the instruments of suicide in fact discourages suicidal behavior.[1] It seems reasonable to suppose that if suicidal individuals lack the means with which to end their lives, they will not do so. The great difficulty here is that human ingenuity makes it possible to end one's life through a vast array of methods, and it seems unlikely that efforts to prevent suicide by restricting access to these methods could possibly succeed. Even if, for example, access to poisons were highly restricted, suicidal individuals could find other methods to end their lives. Moreover, some of the means people use to end their lives are so commonplace that it would seem counterproductive, even crazy, to try to restrict access to them. How realistic is it to try to restrict access to suicidal means such as knives and rope?

That being said, there is a great deal of evidence to suggest that a person's access to lethal means contributes to whether a person tries suicide, irrespective of whether their suicidal act results in their death. As we have noted, how serious a person is about ending her life is a complex matter, and there does not appear to be a simple, linear relationship between seriousness of suicidal intent and the lethality of the methods people use in their suicidal acts. We might naturally expect that people who use suicide methods that are unlikely to actually kill them (cutting themselves, taking large numbers of over-the-counter painkillers) are less serious about wanting to die than people who use highly lethal methods (guns, jumping off tall buildings), but this is not the case. When asked about their chosen method, whether it is guns, poisons, or carbon monoxide, suicide survivors typically say that they chose their method largely because it was available and they *perceived* that method to be lethal. This is not surprising, since the act of suicide itself, though occasionally carefully planned and premeditated, is more often an impulsive conclusion to a pre-existing pattern of suicidal thought. One study conducted in Houston, Texas, asked suicidal individuals who survived their attempts at death how much time passed between the time they decided to end their lives and the actual suicide attempt. Nearly a quarter said less than five minutes, and nearly three-quarters said less than one hour. As a result, most suicidal people seem to give relatively little thought to the means they will use and generally do not go to great lengths in order to secure

---

1   The statistical information in this section is drawn from the Harvard School of Public Health "Means Matter" website: http://www.meansmatter.org.

the means they might prefer to use. Hence, people will typically use those lethal means that are ready to hand. Often, by the time an individual might decide to switch from one suicide method to another, the desire to commit suicide has already ebbed. On top of that, our beliefs about just how lethal various methods are tend to be wildly off base, in particular the gross overestimation of how deadly cutting oneself or taking non-prescription drugs actually is.

Taken together, these considerations suggest that restricting suicidal means will tend to reduce the number of suicidal deaths because, by and large, suicidal people do not rationally select their suicide methods, nor do they tend to "substitute" one method when their chosen method is unavailable. Restricting access to a highly lethal means of death would thus reduce the probability of suicidal death, and, in fact, a number of societies have successfully cut their rates of suicide by restricting access to popular and potent suicide methods. In many poorer countries, pesticides and other poisonous agricultural chemicals have been common suicide methods, but nations such as Samoa have reduced their suicide rates dramatically by pulling these products from the market. Prior to the 1950s, inhaling gas from household stoves was the most common suicide method in England. This gas, derived from coal, contained 10 to 20 per cent carbon monoxide and was therefore highly lethal. Over a two-decade span, coal-based stove gas was phased out in favor of natural gas, which contains only a minuscule amount of carbon monoxide. Suicides in England due to carbon monoxide poisoning fell dramatically, and though the number of suicides via other methods increased slightly, the net effect was to decrease suicide overall. Some experts estimate that over 30,000 lives were saved by changing the composition of English stove gas. Given this evidence, restricting access to the means of death is likely to diminish the number of suicides. It does so not by treating mental illness or by diminishing suicidal thoughts; rather, restricting access to these means prevents suicide from leading to death and makes suicide attempts less lethal.

Of all the lethal means people use to end their lives, guns have proven to be the most controversial, especially in the United States, which is distinctive among Western nations in having a strong gun culture and widespread gun ownership. Opponents of laws restricting gun access and ownership point out that the rate of suicide in countries that have high levels of gun ownership, such as the US, are no higher than in countries that have low levels of gun ownership, thus suggesting that the prevalence of guns in a society does not correlate with its rates of suicide. However, it is difficult to deny that guns play a large role in American suicides. About half of all gun deaths in the US are suicides, guns are the most common method of suicide in the US, and more people die from suicides due to guns than from all other suicide methods put together. It would of course be facile to say that guns *cause* suicide; it is very unlikely that merely having access to guns, or having access to any lethal means, will turn a non-suicidal person into a suicidal person. Nor is it likely that gun owners are more commonly suicidal than non-gun owners.

Nevertheless, guns have certain features that make them an especially good way to kill oneself. First, guns are excellent killers. A 2004 study conducted for the Centers for Disease Control found that 85 per cent of incidents where a person attempted to harm herself using a gun were fatal. In contrast, only 31 per cent of self-inflicted falls were fatal, and just one or two per cent of attempts to die by poisoning oneself or by cutting oneself proved fatal.[1] Guns inflict massive tissue damage and severe bleeding, making them well suited for suicide attempts. Few gunshot victims recover from their wounds, despite the best efforts of emergency room doctors. Guns also act so quickly to produce death that a suicidal person does not have the opportunity to reconsider the act. Other suicide methods (e.g., attempted poisoning and hanging) can sometimes be stopped mid-attempt if a person opts to stay alive, but it is awfully difficult to intervene when one shoots oneself. Finally, operating a gun takes fairly little expertise: a person can end her life with a gun simply by pulling a trigger, without having to know how to tie a noose or measure a lethal drug overdose.

The high lethality of guns suggests that reducing access to them would decrease rates of suicide. Again, although there does not appear to be a simple correlation between access to guns and the frequency of suicide, there are reasons to think that restricting access to guns would have a positive effect on the suicide rate. Evidence for this can be found in empirical studies that have concluded that within the US, suicide rates tend to be higher in states with higher levels of gun ownership.[2] Furthermore, suicide rates in Austria dropped after its government passed strict gun laws in 1997.[3]

---

1   A. Vyrostek, J.L. Annest, and G.W. Ryan, "Surveillance for fatal and nonfatal injuries—United States, 2001." *Morbidity and Mortality Weekly Report* 53 (SS07) (2004): 1-57 (http://www.cdc.gov/mmwr/preview/mmwrhtml/ss5307a1.htm).
2   See Harvard School of Public Health, "Means Matter," ("Gun Prevalence and Suicide Rank by State," http://www.hsph.harvard.edu/news/hphr/social-health-hazards/spr08gunprevalence/).
3   See N.D. Kapusta, E. Etzersdorfer, C. Krall, and G. Sonneck, "Firearm legislation reform in the European Union: impact on firearm availability, firearm suicide and homicide rates in Austria," *British Journal of Psychiatry* 191 (2007): 253-57.

I hesitate to draw dramatic conclusions from this evidence. Yes, restricting access to guns would reduce the suicide rate and prevent many unjustified and unnecessary deaths. However, restricting access to guns must be weighed against the value people attach to owning guns. Many people enjoy hunting or believe that owning a gun makes themselves or their homes more secure against violent crime. These issues are far too great to be broached here, but we should at least be mindful that whatever reduction in suicides results from restricting access to guns ought to be weighed against the perceived benefits of gun ownership. Furthermore, restricting access to guns is more easily said than done, since gun laws are notoriously difficult to enforce. Add to this the fact that there are perhaps 100 million guns in the US, and we might conclude that any effort to restrict access to guns is likely to be unsuccessful. There are simply too many people with too many guns. Finally, I have spoken rather vaguely to this point of "restricting access" to guns. But keep in mind that "restricting access," like that nebulous phrase "gun control," encompasses many different kinds of measures. Yes, we could ban private gun ownership, as a few nations have done. But there may be ways to reduce the number of gun-related suicides with measures that interfere less with people's right to own guns. Stronger safety and storage requirements, such as gun locks and trigger identification mechanisms, might keep guns away from suicidal people. Moreover, laws could prevent those with a history of suicide, or those who live with a person who has such a history, from owning a gun. This sort of targeted legal intervention could be highly effective in reducing gun-related suicides without a sweeping ban on gun ownership.

Conclusion

Thomas Joiner has observed that clinicians often display one or more unhelpful attitudes toward stopping suicide.[1] Some incline toward "alarmism," treating any evidence whatsoever that a person is contemplating or intending suicide as a life-threatening emergency demanding that some means of intervention be pursued. Better safe than sorry, say the alarmists. On the other side, Joiner observes those whose attitudes toward suicide are "dismissive," treating most suicidal thought and behavior as nothing more than a childish bid for

---

1   *Why People Die by Suicide* (Cambridge, MA: Harvard University Press, 2007), pp. 18–22.

attention. In his estimation, both of these approaches are clinically unsound. I have tried here to argue that both approaches are also morally suspect, inviting either overreaction that wrongs individuals or underreaction that is not sufficiently sensitive to the psychological realities of suicidal behavior. Some of the most effective measures we might take to reduce suicide fall outside the clinical context in any case. Efforts to educate the public and medical professionals about suicide, as well as efforts to restrict access to guns and other lethal suicide methods, are likely to be the most effective ways to reduce suicide in the aggregate.

Further Reading

Comparatively speaking, philosophers have said little about our duties toward the suicidal. Victor Cosculluela (1994) addresses the question, as do I in Cholbi (2002). Battin (2005) defends an "err on the side of life" approach to suicide intervention, similar to the one I defend in this chapter. Joiner (2007) is the best recent investigation of the causes of suicide and thus has a great deal of relevance to questions surrounding intervention. Jamison (2000) is also useful in this regard. Harvard University's School of Public Health has an outstanding website, Means Matter (http://www.meansmatter.org), which investigates the relationship between suicidal behavior and the availability of different suicide methods and measures. Dresser (1984) provides a valuable introduction to Ulysses contracts. Some useful discussions and defense of such contracts are found in Halpern and Szmukler (1997) and Spellecy (2003).

six

Assisted Suicide

In an age of increased longevity and medical advances, death can be suspended, sometimes indefinitely, and no longer slips in according to its own immutable timetable.[1]

THE LAST HALF-CENTURY HAS witnessed an explosion in public and academic interest in ethical questions related to both the extending and ending of life. Indeed, a whole academic subfield of biomedical ethics has arisen in no small measure to investigate such questions. And the most heated debates have concerned whether individuals have a right to be aided in their efforts to end their lives—whether there is, so to speak, a right to assisted suicide. That is the topic of this chapter.

A Duty to Assist Suicide?

Let us approach this question from two ends, so to speak, and work toward the murky middle. A suicidal act is morally impermissible, permissible but

---

1   *Los Angeles Times*, Editorial: "Planning for worse than taxes," 22 March 2005 (http://articles.latimes.com/2005/mar/22/opinion/ed-wills22).

not required, or required. The first category can be dealt with readily. If an individual's suicidal act were morally impermissible, then it would be morally impermissible for others knowingly to assist that person to end her life. This is an instance of a more general moral premise that seems inarguable: it is wrong to assist someone else in doing what is wrong. Note that this is a claim about whether it is permissible to *aid* people in doing what is impermissible, not a claim about whether it is permissible to *prevent* people from doing what is impermissible; as I argued in Chapter Four, it does not follow merely from the fact that someone else intends to do something morally wrong that we are always allowed to stop her from doing so. For example, aiding another person in performing a criminal wrong is itself wrong; helping someone sell goods you know to be stolen or helping someone kill his spouse is but one step removed from doing it oneself. Whether this situation is applicable in the case of suicide depends on whether suicide is morally impermissible, which itself is a controversial question, as we discovered in Chapter Two. But *if* a suicidal act is morally impermissible, knowingly assisting in that act is impermissible too.

At the other end of the spectrum, assisting someone whose suicide is morally required is at least morally permissible. Again, this follows from a more general moral principle, namely that it is not wrong to aid others in doing what is morally required. Of course, given the skeptical conclusions about the duty to die that we reached in Chapter Four, there may be very few opportunities to assist someone in fulfilling such a duty. Why is it only morally permissible, rather than morally required, to aid someone whose suicide is morally required? In some cases, we may not be in a position to aid. I have little ability to aid in the morally required suicide of a person living in central Asia, for instance. In other cases, we may have other moral obligations that conflict with aiding someone's suicide. Many medical professionals, for example, believe that their obligations to their patients are to heal and to provide comfort, but never to participate in their deaths. If this is correct, then it would be wrong for medical professionals to assist their patients in committing suicide, even if that suicide is morally required. (We will return to the issue of the role of medical professionals in assisting suicide later in this chapter.)

The more intriguing question is therefore whether, when a suicidal act is merely permissible, we are ever morally required to aid in that suicide. To hone in on this question, I will invoke a distinction already familiar from Chapter Two. Some of the moral obligations we owe to others are *general* in that they do not depend on any specific relationship we bear to them. I ought not to assault others or lie to them, simply because those are the duties I owe to everyone, not because of any relationship that exists between me and specific others. Other obligations are *role-specific* because they depend on some specific relationship we bear to them. The most familiar examples of role-specific obligations are those arising from professional relationships, such as the obligations that doctors owe their patients or that police officers owe the public, familial relationships, and friendships. For the most part, we do not, I would suggest, have a duty to aid in the suicides of those to whom we bear no specific relationship. For one thing, those to whom we bear no specific moral relationship are not likely to seek our aid in ending their lives and so we would be in no position to fulfill the duty. After all, we are little better than strangers to one another. Strangers are certainly *permitted* to aid other strangers, but only in exceptional circumstances is such aid required. (I might have a duty to aid a stranger in peril if I am the only one who could provide such aid, as Singer's "drowning child" example illustrates.) What can transform a mere permission to aid in another's suicide is the presence of a role obligation, for often, aid that would be merely permissible on the part of a stranger is morally obligatory on the part of someone with whom we have a specific role relationship. Parents are required to aid their children in ways that mere strangers are merely permitted to aid them. So too are medical professionals required to help those who are ill, whereas strangers are merely permitted to help.

Let us consider these role relationships in turn and examine whether they ground a requirement to assist others in their morally permissible suicides. Do family members or friends of suicidal individuals have an obligation to aid, assuming the suicide in question is at least morally permissible? The duties that friends and family owe one another are doubtless very complex, and I make no pretense of summarizing or adequately accounting for those duties here. Rather, the more economical approach is to ask whether there are duties that friends and family members owe one another that would imply a duty to aid in suicide. It is clear, though, that friends and family members owe one another various duties that might imply a duty to aid in one another's suicides. Friends and family have duties to promote one another's well-being and to treat one another compassionately. Their duties in these areas are distinctive in that these are not simply duties not to harm, but positive duties to actively seek out ways to promote one another's welfare.

However, friends and family members often lack two attributes crucial to the duty to aid in suicide: competence and available means. Methods of committing suicide vary, as do the ways in which another person might aid in suicide. Those who commit suicide in the typical fashion can use a variety of methods, but many of these methods are unreliable (e.g., over-the-counter drugs), gruesome (e.g., stabbing, shooting), or unavailable to all but doctors (e.g., prescription drugs). Friends and family members may be capable of providing certain forms of assistance to those seeking to end their lives, but they are likely to be neither sufficiently knowledgeable about how to bring about death effectively and in accordance with their loved one's desires nor in a position to acquire the materials needed to aid another person in dying. The consequences of not providing adequate assistance can be serious: a botched suicide can leave a person worse off than she was before.

Physician-assisted Suicide

In contrast, concerns about the competence of those who aid and the availability of lethal materials provides a reason to think that another group of individuals—medical professionals—may be uniquely situated to aid in suicide. In contemporary societies, the medical profession has a legal monopoly on the desirable means of bringing about one's own death. Those in the medical profession, by virtue of their knowledge of how to keep people alive, also have expertise in how to bring about death in ways that are hygienic, reliable, and low in trauma. Whether or not members of the medical profession should have this monopoly, it could be argued that they are the only individuals who should be assisting in suicide. Anyone else lacks the relevant expertise and could easily botch the suicide attempt, with dire consequences for the suicidal individual.

Yet many doctors and nurses have strong reservations about involving themselves in their patients' desire to end their own lives. Inevitably, the attitudes of medical personnel toward assisted suicide will reflect the broader attitudes of the societies in which they live, and as attitudes toward assisted suicide have become more permissive, physicians' attitudes toward it have loosened as well. However, many studies of medical personnel suggest that physicians have greater reservations about assisted suicide than does the general public. In both the United States and the United Kingdom, a solid majority of the public supports patients with terminal illnesses having the legal right to seek physicians' assistance in dying.[1] Surveys of physicians have generally put support for the legalization of physician-assisted suicide at less than half.[2]

Self-interest partially explains the reservations about assisted suicide among medical professionals. Understandably, they do not want to be held morally or legally responsible for a person's death. (Except in three states, assisted suicide is illegal in the US, and it remains illegal in many nations throughout the world.) Moreover, many physicians, not wanting to "play God" or to lay themselves open to the charge of abusing their authority, prefer not to be given much of a say in whether a patient dies and thus try to remain impartial on the issue of assisted suicide. Medical personnel express a variety of concerns about assisted suicide, holding that assisted suicide is defensible if the individual provides consent to dying, but they fear that in actual cases it can be difficult to determine whether the patient is either competent to give consent or has already fully consented.

These prudential and pragmatic concerns aside, some medical professionals appear to rest their views of assisted suicide on distinctions that, in many people's minds, are morally trivial. Though many medical professionals oppose assisted suicide, the overwhelming majority believe that patients (at least when competent) have a moral right to refuse treatment, including life support, and that medical professionals must honor patients' requests to refuse life-extending treatment. Withdrawing or not providing medical treatments that would extend life with the intention of bringing about a patient's death is often termed *passive euthanasia*, and when this occurs with the patient's

---

1   See J.E. Seymour, J. French, and E. Richardson, "Dying matters: Let's talk about it," *BMJ* 341 (2010): 4860; D. Badcott, "Assisted dying: the influence of public opinion in an increasingly diverse society." *Medicine, Health Care, and Philosophy* 13 (2010): 389-97; and BBC World News America/Harris Poll (2011), "Large Majorities Support Doctor Assisted Suicide for Terminally Ill Patients in Great Pain" (http://www.harrisinteractive.com/vault/HI-Harris-Poll-BBC-Doctor-Suicide-2011-01-25.pdf).

2   See C. Seale, "Legalisation of euthanasia or physician-assisted suicide: survey of doctors' attitudes," *Palliative Medicine* 23 (2009): 205-12; T. Hussain and P. White, "GPs' views on the practice of physician-assisted suicide and their role in proposed UK legalisation: a qualitative study," *British Journal of General Practice* 59 (2009): 844-49; and W. Lee, A. Price, L. Rayner, L., and M. Hotpof, "Survey of doctors' opinions of the legalization of physician assisted suicide," *BMC Medical Ethics* 10.2 (2009) (http://www.biomedcentral.com/1472-6939/10/2).

consent, *voluntary* passive euthanasia. Many medical professionals seem to draw a moral boundary between voluntary passive euthanasia and assisting a consenting patient by enabling her suicide.

In both passive euthanasia and assisted suicide, the patient intentionally instigates a chain of events that knowingly leads to her own death, with the medical professional playing an indispensable role in instigating that chain of events. What, if anything, differentiates these two situations? The difference is in the causal pathway leading to death. When a physician removes a patient from life support, what kills the patient is her underlying illness (advanced cancer, for instance), whereas when a physician provides a lethal drug that a patient then uses to end her life, the patient dies from a lethal drug overdose facilitated by the physician. Many physicians apparently believe that this difference in the causal mechanism of death is morally significant, such that voluntary passive euthanasia is morally permissible but assisted suicide is not. There is, from this perspective, a morally important difference between allowing a patient to die and helping a patient kill herself.

However, I contend that this is at best controversial. In both cases, the morally salient facts appear the same: a physician knowingly aids in bringing about a patient's death with the patient's consent. Indeed, it could be argued that in some of the former cases—of agreeing not to provide or continue life-sustaining treatment—a medical professional is more central to the patient's cause of death than in the latter cases, so ending or denying life-sustaining treatment is morally *worse* than providing a patient with lethal materials. After all, in ending life-sustaining treatment, a medical professional may have to deliberately act so as to intervene to produce death; a physician may literally have to "pull the plug." In contrast, when a physician prescribes a patient a suicidal dose of drugs, the control over the patient's death ultimately rests with her, since it is her deliberate act of taking the drug that results in her death. In any event, the distinction between honoring a patient's request to refuse treatment—voluntary passive euthanasia—and honoring her request to provide the means by which she can end her life—assisted suicide—does not have the straightforward moral significance that many medical professionals evidently believe it does.

On top of that, even if this distinction is morally significant, its significance may not support the thesis that not treating a patient (or honoring a patient's refusal of treatment) with lethal results is morally *better* than helping the patient to end his life. Imagine that a patient with cancer tells his physician that he is undergoing unbearable pain and wishes to die. The physician works in a jurisdiction where not only may she honor a patient's request not to treat his condition or to continue life-sustaining measures, but she may also provide the patient with a lethal dose of drugs that the patient may administer himself. Which of these measures, each of which is sufficient to lead to the patient's death, is morally preferable? Obviously, the details of the situation matter a great deal here, but it will often be true that providing the patient with the lethal dose is better for the patient's welfare than stopping the life-sustaining measures or not providing life-extending treatments. A patient who has a lethal dose of medicine available to him can use the dose when he sees fit, and death will be rapid and painless. He could choose to die tomorrow, next week, next month, or so on. In contrast, suppose the physician simply stops treating the patient's cancer and the patient dies of his underlying condition; such a death will often be slower, more painful, and more psychologically trying for all concerned. In such situations, physicians should provide the best pain relief available, but even the best measures may still leave the patient in pain, debilitated, or nearly unconscious. To many, it becomes hard to see, whatever moral difference there might be between voluntary passive euthanasia and assisted suicide, how the former is superior to the latter in *all* cases. Compassionate concern for the patient's welfare seems to dictate that assisting the patient to die through direct measures rather than "letting nature take its course" can be more humane. Thus, physicians and medical professionals, who all have a duty to act in their patients' interests, may want to rethink whether this distinction can support a strong argument for honoring patients' refusals of treatment but not their requests for aid in dying.

The healing ethic and the caretaker ethic

Some medical professionals invoke the problematic distinction between voluntary passive euthanasia and assisted suicide in order to justify their opposition to physician-assisted suicide. I would suggest, however, that at the heart of most medical professionals' reservations about assisting in suicide is the perception that assisted suicide runs contrary to an ethical self-conception shared by many in medicine. Perhaps the most interesting finding in surveys of physicians' attitudes toward assisted suicide is the discrepancy between, on the one hand, their support *in principle* for assisted suicide and, on the other hand, their having actually assisted in suicide or their willingness to do so. A larger number of physicians support assisted suicide than have either assisted in a suicide or would be willing to do so (though the number of physicians who have participated in assisted suicide or euthanasia is larger than one might expect[1]). This implies an anxiety, not about assisted suicide as such, but about the role of physicians in assisting in suicide. Many medical professionals subscribe to a medical ethic that we might call the *healing ethic*, according to which they have an obligation not to harm their patients and, more specifically, to treat their illnesses and extend their lives. Furthermore, the healing ethic sees the obligations not to harm patients as the cornerstone of the trust that ought to exist between patients and their medical care providers. This healing ethic is reflected in the well-known Hippocratic Oath, taken by physicians upon entering the medical profession.

There are two ways in which assisted suicide appears incompatible with the healing ethic. Obviously, if the moral obligation of medical professionals is to heal and to extend life, then assisting a patient to end her life is contrary to their moral obligations. Second, many physicians believe that if they were to participate in assisted suicides, they would undermine their patients' confidence in their dedication to their patients' health.

Let us take these worries in turn. Would the involvement of medical professionals in assisted suicide undermine patients' faith in those professionals as healers? The philosopher Bernard Baumrin forcefully articulates that it would:

> Doctors must not engage in assisting suicide. They are inheritors of a valuable tradition that inspires public trust. None should be even partly responsible for the erosion of that trust. Nothing that is remotely beneficial to some particular patient *in extremis* is worth the damage that will be created by the perception that physicians sometimes aid and even abet people in taking their own lives.[2]

To know that one's doctor has at some point helped other patients to die might change a patient's perception of the doctor's role in the doctor-patient

---

1   Charles H. Baron, "Hastening death: the seven deadly sins of the status quo," in T.E. Quill and M.P. Battin (eds.), *Physician-Assisted Dying: The Case for Palliative Care and Patient Choice* (Baltimore: Johns Hopkins University Press, 2004), p. 314.

2   "Doctor, stay thy hand," in M.P. Battin, R. Rhodes, and A. Silvers (eds.), *Physician-Assisted Suicide: Expanding the Debate* (New York: Routledge, 1998), p. 181.

relationship. But it is not obvious that Baumrin is correct in concluding that it would change that perception for the worse or, more exactly, that it would undermine a patient's trust in the doctor. For some patients, knowing that one's doctor would, at some future time, be willing to assist in suicide may come as a relief. The alternative, after all, could be that a doctor would be adamant on keeping a patient alive regardless of his level of suffering or his quality of life. For many patients, that frightening prospect would do more to undermine their trust in their doctors than would a knowledge of the doctor's willingness to assist in suicide. Furthermore, steps can be taken that would mitigate the chances that the doctor-patient relationship would erode if physicians could participate in their patients' death. Those states and countries in which physician-assisted suicide is legal generally have procedural safeguards that are intended, among other things, to ensure that patients' trust in their care providers will not be abused or undermined. For example, most of the jurisdictions that permit physician-assisted suicide require a "second opinion": a patient diagnosed with a terminal or highly painful illness must have that diagnosis confirmed by a second physician and requires multiple acts of consent by the patient, the presence of neutral witnesses, and so on. Some jurisdictions also try to maintain the physician's distance from the actual act of killing the patient by allowing physicians to prescribe a lethal drug to patients but prohibiting them from actually administering the drug themselves. The first worry might also be alleviated if the health care system introduced a class of medical professionals with special responsibility for, and expertise in, assisted dying. The availability of such professionals—"suicide aides" or "euthanists," we might call them—might make assisted suicide possible without compromising physicians' ethics or the trust that grounds their relationships with their patients.

The second worry does not hinge on matters of fact but on sheer logic. The healing ethic is logically incompatible with medical professionals' assisting in suicide. To assist in killing is diametrically opposed to healing and extending life. Answering this worry thus requires an assessment of the healing ethic itself. Should medical professionals give healing of illness and the extension of life such a central place in their ethical self-conception? Are there other ways of understanding their obligations to their patients that might license their assisting in suicide? In recent decades, some patients have begun to think of their doctors not simply in terms of their role as healers and extenders of life, but also as guardians of their happiness, autonomy, and lifestyle. On the conception of the ethics of medical professionals—call it the *caretaker ethic*—healing patients of disease and extending their lives continue to be central obligations of medical professionals. However, these obligations coexist with, and must sometimes take a back seat to, obligations to provide patients with a positive quality of life for as long as doing so is feasible. Physicians, nurses, and other health-care professionals are thus as much advisors who cooperate with patients in pursuing a worthwhile life as they are healers who keep disease and death at bay.

My own guess would be that many medical professionals view their obligations to their patients in terms of a blend of these two ethical outlooks, and deciding between the healing ethic and the caretaker ethic is much too large a project to be undertaken here. I note only that the caretaker ethic is likely to be more sympathetic to medical professionals' participation in their patients' suicides. For at least a small number of patients, ending their lives sooner than the progress of nature would be a way of preserving or providing a sense of greater autonomy, happiness, or quality of life. Clearly, for medical professionals, including those operating under the caretaker ethic, deciding when a patient's life is best brought to an end is a difficult decision (and not one for them to make on their own in any case). But the caretaker ethic, unlike the healing ethic, allows that sometimes medical professionals' obligations are *not* to heal illness or to extend life. This position would seem to open the door to medical professionals aiding in others' suicides.

Aiding Suicide and the Slippery Slope

For some, the arguments of the previous sections are beside the point: even if it is true that aiding others to end their lives is at least sometimes morally permissible, they say, we should nevertheless act *as if* it were not. For these critics, allowing assisted suicide will have many unintended consequences that would, morally speaking, be far worse than the good consequences that might flow from allowing it. More specifically, these critics argue that we will not be able to fashion a system to permit only those physician-assisted suicides that are morally justified; instead, many horrible moral wrongs will occur. This is an excellent example of a so-called "slippery slope" objection. Imagine that a boulder sits precariously atop a tall plateau. When pushed ever so slightly over the edge of that plateau, the boulder will descend down the slope, rapidly picking up speed. Those who use the slippery slope objection have in mind that the present situation (except in all but a few states and countries) corresponds to the boulder sitting stably atop the plateau. But once we permit physician-assisted suicide, even under stringent conditions, the boulder moves down the slope toward more morally troubling outcomes. Note that the objection does not directly contest the thesis; that is, it does not actually claim that it is false that aiding others' suicides is morally permissible. Rather, it proposes that the acceptance of this thesis will have dire moral consequences. The thesis itself, according to this objection, is benign. Believing it, on the other hand, is morally worrisome because we will inevitably end up in a situation that, morally speaking, is far worse than the status quo.

The mere image or suggestion of the slippery slope is not enough for us to evaluate a slippery slope argument, however. We need to know what the slippery slope objectors believe is slippery about the slope and, more specifically, what awful moral consequences are at its bottom. Opponents of assisted suicide have had in mind two distinct slippery slopes. The first I will call the *conceptual slope*. Assisted suicide may be acceptable in some circumstances, but permitting it will lead people to believe that they have a right to aid others in dying, but because people are often selfish or lack moral virtue, they are likely to abuse the right to assist others in ending their lives. For example, the family members of a person whose suicide would be irrational may become weary of caring for her. They may invoke the claim that they have an obligation to aid her to push her to end her life. Or perhaps medical personnel facing a shortage of hospital beds may act clandestinely to bring about a person's death, believing that they are rightly aiding the person in dying. The result of such abuse or bad moral judgment will be that the boundaries between assisted suicide (which we may grant for the sake of argument is morally permissible under some conditions) and other more morally alarming practices will become blurred.

More specifically, critics argue, assisted suicide will first give way to voluntary *active* euthanasia. Voluntary active euthanasia differs from assisted suicide in a significant way: whereas in assisted suicide a physician provides information and/or lethal means to an individual who may then proceed to use that information or means to end her life, in voluntary active euthanasia the physician or medical professional acts to end the patient's life with her informed consent (consent being provided either in the situation in question or by means of an advance directive). Active euthanasia differs from passive

euthanasia (mentioned earlier in this chapter) in that the former involves acting so as to bring about a patient's death, whereas the latter involves not doing
something that would otherwise extend the patient's life. For example, if a
patient requests not to be given food or fluids necessary to keep her alive and
a physician honors this request, the patient dies as a result of voluntary passive
euthanasia. If a patient receives a prescription from her doctor for a lethal dose
of medicine and information on how to administer it, and then proceeds to
take the lethal dose, then assisted suicide has occurred. And if the patient, in
full possession of her rational competence, agrees to let the doctor administer
the lethal dose, then voluntary active euthanasia has occurred.

Many critics of physician-assisted suicide believe that voluntary active
euthanasia is not morally justified even under the conditions under which
assisted suicide is morally justified. To permit assisted suicide, then, opens the
door to a slippery slope toward voluntary active euthanasia. Critics of assisted
suicide then claim that voluntary euthanasia will open the door to *non-voluntary euthanasia*, which occurs when an individual has neither consented to her
being killed nor indicated that she does not wish to be killed (and typically, is
in a coma or other state that prevents her from providing or withholding her
consent to be killed). In considering non-voluntary euthanasia, we are literally
working in the dark, with no evidence concerning the patient's wish to die.

Non-voluntary euthanasia involves killing individuals without their consent and is morally troubling for that reason. Worse still, according to these
critics, the slope is slippery enough that an even more alarming practice will
arise: *involuntary euthanasia.* Involuntary euthanasia is like voluntary euthanasia in that an individual dies not by causing her own death directly, but
by someone else causing her death. However, involuntary euthanasia occurs
when a person has indicated a rational preference *not* to be killed. Critics of
assisted suicide understandably see involuntary euthanasia as tantamount to
murder. Hence, if the conceptual slope is slippery, the result will be not only
some acts of morally permissible assisted suicide, but also many increasingly
horrible acts of voluntary, non-voluntary, and involuntary euthanasia.

The second alleged slippery slope I will call the *victim slope.* This slope
expresses the worry that permitting assisted suicide for competent patients
will put pressure on certain vulnerable groups to accept assisted suicide. Judge
Robert Beezer, writing a dissenting opinion in a 1996 case, articulated the
victim slope reasoning well. He wrote that legal acknowledgment of a right to
assisted suicide

might spawn pressure on the elderly and infirm—but still happily alive—to "die and get out of the way." Also at risk are the poor and minorities, who have been shown to suffer more pain (i.e. they receive less treatment for their pain) than other groups.... Further, like the elderly and infirm, they, as well as the handicapped, are at risk of being unwanted and subjected to pressure to choose physician-assisted suicide rather than continued treatment. ... The poor, the elderly, the disabled and minorities are all at risk from undue pressure to commit physician-assisted suicide, either through direct pressure or through inadequate treatment of their pain and suffering. The only way to achieve adequate protection for these groups is to maintain a bright-line rule against physician-assisted suicide.[1]

Beezer argues that if physician assisted suicide were accepted and practiced, certain groups—the poor, the uninsured, the elderly, the disabled, and minorities—might find themselves subtly pressured to seek assisted suicide. The lives of members of groups at the periphery of society might, in effect, not be valued as highly as other lives. Moreover, these groups may not have their pain or illnesses treated as effectively as others and so might have better reason to seek out assisted suicide. As I read Beezer, his worry is not that it is unjust *per se* that members of some groups might be more likely to seek assisted suicide than others; in fact, it would be very surprising if some groups (e.g., those with diagnosed cancers) were not especially likely to seek assisted suicide. Beezer's concern is rather that a person's poverty, disability or membership in a minority group should not influence whether that person opts for assisted suicide. Those facts ought not to matter in deciding whether to seek out assisted suicide, but (Beezer argues) they will in fact turn out to matter, with the result that many people will seek out assisted suicide for the wrong reasons. People in these vulnerable groups will opt for assisted suicide more commonly than they should and for reasons unrelated to the moral reasons that support a right to assisted suicide. That, Beezer believes, is sufficient grounds not to permit assisted suicide at all—that we should maintain a "bright-line rule" against it.

Taken together, the conceptual and victim slippery slopes paint a frightening picture of the unintended consequences of permitting assisted suicide.

---

1   *Compassion in Dying v. Washington*, 850 F. Supp. 1454 (1994).

At its worst, opponents imagine that physicians, family members, or government bureaucrats will end up killing people against their will and for society's convenience, with a disproportionate number of those killed being poor, uninsured, elderly, disabled, or of minority status. Some advocates of the slippery slope argument go so far as to claim that permitting assisted suicide is the first step toward the kind of eugenics practiced by the Nazi regime.

Just how slippery are the two slopes?

But are these arguments convincing, or can they be dismissed as rhetorical scare tactics? Slippery slope arguments are common in ethical debates, but evaluating such arguments is tricky. It is certainly *possible* that people could come to accept the thesis that aiding suicide is morally permissible without their abusing or misunderstanding it, extending it disproportionately to disadvantaged or vulnerable groups, but of course that is not what is intended by slippery slope arguments anyway. The force of these arguments depends on psychological and sociological hypotheses about how people's attitudes and behavior change in response to changes in their moral culture. More specifically, the objection contends that if this thesis were widely acknowledged, many people would end up being "helped" to die who ought not to die or whose deaths would be unjust.

It has often been noticed that slippery slope arguments encode a status quo bias. In other words, they are invariably used to argue that some deviation from existing practice or belief is morally troubling and should therefore be avoided. Implicit, then, in such arguments is the belief that the present situation is morally acceptable or, at the very least, clearly better than the nightmare scenario that occupies the bottom of the alleged slippery slope. But that is not obviously the case when it comes to assisted suicide. With few exceptions, suicidal individuals cannot legally enlist the aid of others to end their lives, a fact that has moral costs of its own (e.g., prolonged suffering). And it would be intellectually dishonest for proponents of the slippery slope argument against assisted suicide to offer hypotheses about the consequences if assisted suicide were acknowledged and accepted without at least taking into account the consequences of the status quo. Hence, even if allowing assisted suicide did invite some abuse, this abuse would have to be weighed against the costs of the status quo.

But would allowing assisted suicide invite such abuse? In other words, should we expect that many individuals would die unjustifiably if assisted suicide were legally permitted and regulated? Opponents of assisted suicide should provide "evidence that shows that horrible slope consequences are *likely* to occur," the philosopher R.G. Frey has argued. "The mere possibility that such consequences might occur," as noted earlier, "does not constitute such evidence."[1] Unfortunately, the fact that very few jurisdictions permit assisted suicide makes this a somewhat speculative question. Let us deal in turn with each of the two slippery slope arguments against assisted suicide in order to examine the extent of the slipperiness of their slopes.

As we have noted, assisted suicide is illegal almost everywhere in the United States and in most countries throughout the world, and laws and practices concerning assisted suicide are a bewildering hodgepodge. Some nations (e.g., Ireland, Russia, and Hungary) specifically outlaw, and actively prosecute, assisted suicide. Some nations (e.g., Sweden and Norway) have no specific laws against assisted suicide but will prosecute those who assist by charging them with manslaughter, with being an accessory to murder, or with other criminal offenses. Other nations (e.g., Canada, England, France, and Scotland) that do not classify suicide itself as a crime will nevertheless prosecute those who assist. Some nations (e.g., Uruguay) have officially criminalized assisted suicide but appear to tolerate it in practice. Because of this dizzying array of laws and practices, identifying "laboratories" where the effects of legally permitting assisted suicide could be properly studied has been difficult. Currently, only three national jurisdictions—Belgium, Switzerland, and the Netherlands—and three US states —Oregon, Washington, and Montana—legally permit assisted suicide, but nearly all of the research done on the effects of permitting assisted suicide have focused on the Netherlands and on Oregon, since these are jurisdictions where the practice has been legalized and actually performed in the relatively recent past. In other words, the Netherlands and Oregon make good test cases for investigating the alleged slippery slope effects of permitting assisted suicide because they enable us to investigate its actual consequences. It would not make any sense to investigate assisted suicide in jurisdictions where it has been legally permitted for a long time, since we have little data about assisted suicide prior to its legalization.

---

1   "The fear of a slippery slope," in G. Dworkin, R.G. Frey, and S. Bok, *Euthanasia and Physician-Assisted Suicide: For and Against* (Cambridge: Cambridge University Press, 1998), p. 63.

In the Netherlands, assisted suicide is legally permitted, and voluntary euthanasia, while still technically illegal, is not prosecuted if physicians meet
specific conditions. In particular, the patient's request for euthanasia must be
voluntary and persist over time; the patient must be aware of his or her condition, treatment options, and prognoses; the patient must be over 12 years
old; and two physicians must confirm the patient's diagnosis, prognosis, and
treatment options. Oregon's Death with Dignity Act does not permit voluntary active euthanasia but permits physician-assisted suicide for capable adults
who have been diagnosed with a terminal illness that will kill them within
six months. Patients meeting these and other conditions can be provided a
prescription for a lethal dose of medication that the patient, not the physician,
may then administer.

One central challenge in studying the slippery slope effects of legalizing
assisted suicide is that assisted suicide and euthanasia constitute a very small
number of overall deaths. In the Netherlands, for instance, assisted suicide
and voluntary euthanasia are responsible for less than 2 per cent of all deaths
per year,[1] and in Oregon fewer than 500 people have taken advantage of the
Death with Dignity Act, not even 0.2 per cent of all deaths in the state over
that time period.[2] Social scientists often advise that it is unwise to draw strong
conclusions from rare events. For example, suppose that I teach an unusually
difficult course, in which an A grade is rare. In the fall term, only one student
receives an A, but in the winter term, two students receive A's. On the face of
it, this looks like a dramatic increase in student performance—a 100-per-cent
increase, in fact. But on the other hand, this is clearly misleading. Given the
infrequency of A grades and the fact that any increase in A grades from one
per term will constitute at least a 100-per-cent increase, it would be wrongheaded for me to detect a meaningful trend in student performance from this
information. Hence, it can be misleading to draw large-scale conclusions from
small segments of data.

With these caveats in mind, is there evidence of the conceptual slippery
slope in the Netherlands or in Oregon? Has opening the door to assisted
suicide led to abuses and, more specifically, to voluntary, non-voluntary, and
involuntary euthanasia? This question became embroiled in controversy when

---

1   Battin et al., "Legal physician-assisted dying in Oregon and the Netherlands: evidence
     concerning the impact on patients in 'vulnerable' groups," *Journal of Medical Ethics* 33
     (2007): 591-97.
2   Oregon Department of Human Services, "Death with Dignity Act annual reports,"
     2009 (http://www.oregon.gov/DHS/ph/pas/ar-index.shtml).

the Dutch government released a 1991 report that found that over 1,000 cases of involuntary euthanasia occur each year in the Netherlands.[1] This initially makes it appear as if the fears of the slippery slope are well founded—that assisted suicide has made physicians "too compassionate," such that they are killing people against their will. However, that statistic, in isolation, tells us nothing about the *effects* of permitting assisted suicide on more morally dubious killings. While the finding of 1,000 cases of involuntary euthanasia after the legalization of assisted suicide and voluntary euthanasia is unsettling, especially since involuntary euthanasia is essentially indistinguishable from murder, we lack a reliable baseline from which to determine to that extent, if any, this rate of involuntary euthanasia can even be correlated with the legalization of assisted suicide and voluntary euthanasia.

It would, however, be reasonable to think that rates of euthanasia would be higher in the Netherlands than in countries in which euthanasia and assisted suicide remain illegal, and if so, this would be evidence of the slippery slope effect. Here, again, we find little consensus and much contentiousness. Some studies have concluded that the rates of euthanasia in the Netherlands are no greater than those in other Western nations, but P.J. van der Maas, the author of several of the key studies on the Dutch experience with euthanasia, concludes that rates of euthanasia in the Netherlands are several times greater than those in the US and other demographically and culturally similar industrialized ations.[2] A further complication in evaluating these data is that we have every reason to think that involuntary or non-voluntary euthanasia takes place even where it is illegal. For instance, assisted suicide and euthanasia are illegal almost everywhere in the US, yet about seven per cent of doctors in that country admit to having complied with a patient's request for euthanasia or aid in dying.[3] The relevant question, then, is how frequently involuntary

---

1 This is the widely cited Remmelink report: M.J. Remmelink et al., Medical Decisions About the End of Life, I. Report of the Committee to Study the Medical Practice Concerning Euthanasia. II. The Study for the Committee on Medical Practice Concerning Euthanasia (2 vols.). The Hague, 1991.

2 P.J. van der Maas, J.I.M. van Delden, L. Pijnenborg, and C.W.N. Looman, "Euthanasia and other medical decisions concerning the end of life," *Lancet* 338 (1991): 669-74; and P.J. van der Maas et al., "Euthanasia, physician-assisted suicide, and other medical practices involving the end of life in the Netherlands, 1990-95," *New England Journal of Medicine* 335 (1996): 1699-1705.

3 D.E. Meier, C.A. Emmons, S. Wallenstein, T. Quill, R.S. Morrison, and C.K. Cassel, "A national survey of physician-assisted suicide and euthanasia in the United States," *New England Journal of Medicine* 338 (1998): 1193.

euthanasia occurs in the US, not whether it occurs at all. Of course, physicians have no incentive to report assisted suicide or euthanasia at all in the US, so reliable numbers about its prevalence are unavailable.

The fairest answer to the question of whether the conceptual slippery slope exists—whether assisted suicide leads to morally abhorrent killings—is that we don't know. In fact, what one would hope to be a straightforward empirical question—"Does legally permitting assisted suicide result in more morally unjustified acts of euthanasia?"—turns out to be hopelessly complicated by conflicting analyses, a lack of reliable data, and difficult-to-isolate counterfactuals. Neil Gorsuch, an opponent of assisted suicide, has examined such data and concluded that the existence of the conceptual slippery slope "cannot be ruled out as unreasonable on the available evidence,"[1] but conversely, nor can its existence be *verified* based on the available evidence.

Then what of the second slippery slope we identified—the victim slope, which suggests that the option of assisted suicide will result in more members of vulnerable groups choosing it? Is there evidence supporting this contention? This slippery slope has been studied less than the conceptual slope, but a provisional answer is "no": the availability of assisted suicide does not put undue pressure on the poor, the elderly, the uninsured, the disabled, or members of ethnic minority groups.

A 2007 study published by Margaret Battin and her colleagues considered publicly available data collected over a twenty-year period in the Netherlands and over an eight-year period in Oregon. The study considered ten vulnerable groups and found "no evidence of heightened risk for the elderly, women, the uninsured, people with low educational status, the poor, the physically disabled or chronically ill, minors, people with psychiatric illnesses including depression, or racial or ethnic minorities, compared with background populations."[2] Indeed, the study found no discernible patterns in the data concerning who sought assisted suicide, aside from the fact that AIDS patients sought it in slightly higher numbers than did those with other terminal conditions. Although this is the most comprehensive study of the victim slope, opponents of assisted suicide dismissed the study on both spurious grounds (i.e., questioning the integrity of the lead author, bioethicist Margaret Battin) and

---

1   *The Future of Assisted Suicide and Euthanasia* (Princeton: Princeton University Press, 2006), p. 142.

2   Battin et al., p. 593.

somewhat more legitimate grounds (i.e., that the study relied on physicians reporting assisted suicides, which may be unreliable). Of course, the study concludes only that there is "no evidence" of the victim slope, but we should remind ourselves of what we can reasonably expect from such studies and where the burden of proof lies. Proving a negative is very difficult, as any researcher can attest. Hence, it is unreasonable to expect that data will disprove the existence of this slippery slope, and, echoing Frey's remark above, it will not do for advocates of a slippery slope to postulate the possibility of such a slope as a compelling reason to accept its existence.

Provisionally, then, in the absence of further evidence, we should be uncertain about whether the conceptual slippery slope exists and outright skeptical that the victim slippery slope exists. Of course, we ought not to foreclose the possibility that additional evidence will emerge that *does* suggest their existence. At the very least, though, the existing evidence quells the worry that permitting assisted suicide puts us on the road to a Nazi-like eugenic nightmare.

Costs, Benefits, and Institutional Design

Behind the slippery slope worries about assisted suicide is a simple-minded view about how social institutions operate. It is tempting to want a legal or social apparatus that will permit only those assisted suicides that are morally justified—the "perfect system," if you will. But this is a vain hope. No complex set of practices or institutions, no matter how carefully or rationally designed, is perfect in this way. Such fallibility is the byproduct of the fact that these practices and institutions are human institutions, overseen and implemented by fallible human beings. Thus, the very best systems of criminal justice occasionally fail to convict guilty defendants (and convict innocent ones). The very best systems to test food products sometimes do not identify tainted food. The very best system permitting assisted suicide would at least sometimes be abused or result in unjustified suicides. It would be unreasonable, then, to hold assisted suicide to an impossibly high standard: that we should reject any set of laws, regulations, and practices unless it allows only those suicides in which the assistance is morally justified.

Instead, we are left with a highly contentious matter of moral judgment. With respect to any given set of laws, regulations, and practices, how do its moral costs (in terms of unjustified deaths, for example) compare to its benefits (reduced pain, suffering, indignity, etc.)? Our aim in creating a set of laws and regulations should be to minimize costs while still securing the intended benefits of those laws and regulations so that the costs are far smaller than the benefits. I have already suggested in my critique of the slippery slope arguments against assisted suicide that the moral costs of assisted suicide are probably less than its critics fear, and even granting that there are costs, these must be weighed against the benefits of permitting assisted suicide. Suppose that for every morally defensible assisted suicide that occurs under a given legal and social regime, one morally indefensible killing (a non-consensual involuntary euthanasia, say) thereby took place that would not have taken place under a less permissive regime. That, many would say, is too steep a moral price to pay for the goods provided by assisted suicide. Some studies of the Dutch system of assisted suicide and euthanasia have found that four acts of voluntary euthanasia or assisted suicide occur for each case of someone being killed without her consent. Is that ratio enough to justify allowing assisted suicide? What if the ratio in question were 100 to one? I am not proposing that we should evaluate these tradeoffs in the crudest numerical or utilitarian terms. I merely point out that even *if* permitting assisted suicide had *some* bad moral results, we should not simply overlook the good moral results of permitting it and suppose that we have offered a watertight argument against assisted suicide.

The desire to know in advance which set of laws, regulations, and practices concerning assisted suicide would be least open to abuse and thereby ethically justifiable is understandable. However, we often do not fully know in advance how to design laws, regulations, and practices to meet our goals. Indeed, it is a conceit on the part of advocates of the slippery slope argument against allowing assisted suicide that they know enough about possible approaches to assisted suicide to state that every one of those approaches is morally worse than the status quo. I have suggested that they do not know this, but even so, it does not follow that assisted suicide should be permitted under just any set of circumstances. The various jurisdictions that allow assisted suicide explicitly recognize this. The Netherlands, Oregon, and the other jurisdictions that permit assisted suicide do not allow it for just anyone for any reason and in fact have put in place various "procedural safeguards." These include restrictions on who may receive assistance, conditions on the provision of consent, requirements concerning diagnosis, and so on. This fact also tends to weaken the slippery slope arguments against assisted suicide. Such procedural safeguards are designed to introduce friction onto the alleged slope from assisted suicide to involuntary euthanasia, that is, to make possible morally justified assisted suicides while preventing the more morally suspect killings that worry critics of assisted suicide. Perhaps the jurisdictions in question have failed with these procedural safeguards, either by not enforcing them adequately or by failing to identify the best safeguards in the first place, but one reaction to the possibility that assisted suicide introduces a slippery slope is to critically examine the existing safeguards rather than disallowing assisted suicide altogether. In other words, even if existing laws and practices might lead to a slippery slope, perhaps those laws and practices could be reformed to make the slopes less slippery. Unfortunately, this is an alternative that critics of assisted suicide rarely mention. In fact, one of the great defining features of democratic societies is that our laws and practices can be responsive to errors, changing information, and evolving moral sensibilities. Given that legalizing assisted suicide has some benefits, it seems premature to give up on fashioning a system of assisted suicide that minimizes its moral costs.

Lastly, I believe that a further benefit to permitting assisted suicide (and one that speaks against the slippery slope argument) is that allowing assisted suicide, even under a very narrow set of circumstances, opens up dialogue on two fronts. First, having assisted suicide available to individuals compels a discussion with their doctors and loved ones not only about that option, but also about the options with which it is likely to be compared. The legalization and social acceptance of assisted suicide puts it in competition with alternative courses of action that do not involve an individual's suicide, and there is some evidence that the possibility of assisted suicide appears to motivate changes in the alternatives to assisted suicide that make the alternatives themselves more attractive. More specifically, it can spur improvements in medical care, particularly palliative and hospice care, which undermine some of the rationales that individuals often have for desiring assisted suicide in the first place. Paradoxically, the availability of assisted suicide could make it less appealing.

More generally, allowing assisted suicide also encourages honest dialogue about how people should end their lives. As I have noted several times in this book, serious and honest discussion about suicide is rare, even in enlightened circles. "Suicide is a whispered word, inappropriate for polite company," writes physician and rabbi Earl Grollman. "Family and friends often pretend they do not hear the word's dread sound even when it is uttered."[1] Surely it would be salutary if the possibility of suicide, assisted or otherwise, could at least be discussed more openly. Too often we assume that discussion of an option will inadvertently encourage that option (in the way that critics of sex education for teenagers argue that it inadvertently encourages sexual promiscuity). In contrast, I propose that the present situation, in which suicide itself is viewed shamefully and assisted suicide is almost universally illegal, isolates suicidal people and probably encourages desperate behavior. For those considering assisted suicide, thoughtful interaction with others about their decision often has little point in the current situation, since assisted suicide is often illegal anyway. The desire to end one's life is often fleeting, confined to a short stage of a person's life. Merely being able to discuss suicidal thoughts is often the simplest and most powerful preventive measure we can take, serving not simply to distract suicidal individuals from their life-ending impulses but providing them with a sense that they are not alone in the world. Furthermore, as I have argued, many of the hardest ethical questions surrounding suicide stem from the all-too-common prospect that the states of mind associated with suicidal ideation render people insufficiently rational with respect to their decision to end their lives. Perhaps the easiest way to counter these irrational tendencies is to bring them out into the open, where they can be scrutinized and better understood. President Bill Clinton once remarked that his position on abortion was that it ought to be "safe, legal, and rare." I advocate a similar position on suicide and believe that faith in the capacity of dialogue and discussion is more likely to advance that position than is the continued treatment of suicide as a social taboo.

Conclusion

Suicide is rarely morally required, sometimes morally optional, and only occasionally morally impermissible. Though it is clear that there is no obligation to assist in morally impermissible suicides, the question of whether there is an obligation to assist morally required or morally optional suicides turns out to be a tricky one. I have argued that there is no general obligation to assist in such suicides, but particular individuals may have an obligation to assist others

---

1   *Suicide: Prevention, Intervention, Postvention* (Boston: Beacon Press, 1988), p. 1

in their suicidal acts if those individuals stand in certain kinds of relationships to the suicidal person. Family and friends may have such an obligation, but they are likely to lack the knowledge or competence to fulfill it. Therefore, the role of physicians and medical professionals in assisting suicide becomes a central issue in debates about aiding suicide. I have argued that medical professionals have some self-interested reasons for not assisting in suicide, but one moral reason that medical professionals cite for opposing assisted suicide—the boundary between aiding suicide and honoring a patient's refusal of treatment—is problematic. The slippery slope arguments against assisted suicide cannot be refuted exactly, but they should not trouble us as much as their proponents think. Ultimately, the question of physician-assisted suicide can be answered only through a thorough philosophical inquiry into the nature of the values underlying the medical profession and, more exactly, whether participating, even indirectly, in patients' deaths can reflect these values.

Further Reading

The literature on assisted suicide, and physician-assisted suicide in particular, is vast. The exchange among Gerald Dworkin, R.G. Frey, and Sissela Bok (1998) is an excellent overview of the main moral issues. Battin, Rhodes, and Silvers (1998) and Battin's (2005) are also valuable introductions.

Callahan (2005) and Gay-Williams (2011) argue for the moral impermissibility of euthanasia and assisted suicide. In his article in the *Stanford Encyclopedia of Philosophy*, Young (2010) replies to many of the objections to assisted suicide and euthanasia. The "Euthanasia" section of ProCon.org (http://euthanasia.procon.org/) is also an even-handed treatment of the subject.

Epilogue: Why?

LET US CONCLUDE OUR philosophical investigation of suicide with a brief investigation of what may be the most elusive question on the issue: why do people do it? This is a question that many people struggle with. For medical professionals, the question is crucial in determining how best to help suicidal people. For philosophers and ethicists, why people voluntarily end their lives can matter to suicide's morality. For the friends and loved ones of suicidal people, especially those suicidal people who end up achieving their wish to die, wrestling with this question is often the cause of a great deal of anguish and confusion. And of course, the question is of great importance to the very people who contemplate suicide.

Oddly enough, although the "why" question is philosophically meaningful to many people, it is not itself a philosophical question. Philosophers are not typically empirical scientists: they conduct no experiments, do no field work, and gather no data. In this respect, philosophers are no better off than laymen in answering this question. Hence, much of this epilogue will not have a philosophical tone. It will instead focus on the evidence from psychology, psychiatry, and sociology in the hope that some headway can be made in explaining why suicide happens.

Movie and television detectives often try to solve cases by directing their attention to those suspects who had "means, motive, and opportunity." Roughly put, this means that in order for someone to have committed a crime, he must have had a way to commit the crime, a reason to commit the crime, and the chance to commit the crime. Whether or not suicide ought to be criminal, the means/motive/opportunity triad provides a useful lens for explaining suicidal behavior. Let us consider these elements in reverse order.

Opportunity

What could it mean to say that suicidal people need an "opportunity" to commit suicide? The thinking that leads up to an attempted suicide is often very complex, in part because people have a number of different goals or concerns in mind when they engage in suicidal behavior. For one thing, suicidal individuals vary in how seriously committed they are to dying, a consideration that will typically influence the suicide method they choose. Moreover, suicidal individuals vary in how public they wish their suicides to be. Some opt to end their lives alone and in their homes, whereas others choose to jump off skyscrapers, step in front of subway trains, or set themselves ablaze. Some suicidal people choose situations and methods that are, relatively speaking, physiologically trauma-free (e.g., pills, poisons, etc.), whereas others seem to relish having their bodies found with grotesque wounds or other signs of distress.

These facts suggest that what counts for one suicidal individual as an attractive "opportunity" to end her life will not be as attractive to another. This can be explained by the variability of the goals, values, and motives of suicidal people. Consider the contrast between the goals and values reflected by someone who seeks to end his life in a daring act of "suicide by cop" and someone who quietly takes an overdose of sleeping pills in his bedroom. The former suicide is likely to be highly public, drawn out, painful, and violent, with psychological trauma (and perhaps even risk of physical injury) to a large number of people other than the suicidal individual (his friends and loved ones, of course, but also police officers, hostages, and bystanders). The latter suicide is likely to be private, relatively quick and painless, with psychological trauma to a much smaller circle of people. The glaring differences between the goals, values, and motives of these two suicides illustrate how having an opportunity to end one's life is not the same for all people.

Motive

Having an "opportunity" to take one's life does not mean much unless a person already has a motive (broadly speaking, a reason) to take her life. As we saw earlier, it is exceptional when a suicidal individual does *not* suffer from a mental disorder. The relationship between mental disorders and suicide is among the most studied questions in psychiatry, and most studies conclude that upward of 90 per cent of all those who die by suicide were suffering from a mental disorder at the time of death. However, it is dismaying that some mental disorders include suicidal behavior among their diagnostic criteria. Among the criteria for the highly controversial borderline personality disorder, for example, is recurrent suicidal behavior, gestures, threats, or self-mutilating behavior. To the philosopher's eye, this raises the prospect of a circular explanation—of suicidal behavior being explained in terms of conditions that have suicidal behavior as one of their symptoms. Logically speaking, this is troubling. Imagine investigating whether drunk driving causes auto accidents, and suppose that whether or not something *counted* as an auto accident depended in part on whether one of the drivers was drunk. It would then be illogical to say that drunk driving causes auto accidents. Typically, causes and effects are supposed to be distinct kinds of events. But if the fact that a driver was drunk is among the facts that lead us to classify the event as an accident in the first place, then the drunk driving is part of the accident, not its cause. So too if suicide and mental disorder are interdefined in this way: it cannot be true that mental disorders cause suicidal behavior if engaging in suicidal behavior is simply what constitutes the disorder, even in part. Purging suicidal behavior as a diagnostic criterion for mental disorders would thus be a great service to our understanding of the causal relationship between them.

Some advocates for the mentally ill recoil when suicide is associated with mental disorders. In their minds, associating suicide and mental illness reinforces the popular misconception that mentally ill people are untreatable, "crazy," and need to be locked up. I do not disagree that such a misconception persists, unfortunately. Indeed, misconceptions about both suicide and mental disorders are rampant, and perhaps claiming that mental disorders are causally implicated in suicide feeds these misconceptions. As we shall see, I agree with these advocates insofar as it is far too simplistic to say that mental illness is uniquely or solely responsible for suicide; however, ignoring the overwhelming volume of data linking suicide and mental illness is not only intellectually dishonest but possibly also dangerous. The mentally ill, whether or not they are suicidal, deserve our sympathy and support, rather than stigmatization and neglect. But we do neither group any favors by denying this link, even if this denial is motivated by sensitivity and good intentions. If we wish to overcome these misconceptions, let knowledge and understanding, rather than more ignorance, be our weapons against this ignorance.

Of course, saying that mental disorders are common factors in suicidal behavior is a coarse claim, for there are many varieties of mental disorder, and they vary in how much they tend to cause suicide. A number of disorders are known to increase the likelihood of suicidal behavior among their sufferers: panic disorder, substance abuse and addiction, and schizophrenia, for example. In considering which mental disorders are most responsible for suicidal behavior, we must distinguish between two different questions:

1   Which disorders lead to the highest *frequency* of suicidal behavior among those who suffer from them?

2   Which disorders are responsible for the largest *numbers* of suicides?

With respect to the first question, two disorders in particular seem to encourage lethal suicidal behavior. The first is the aforementioned borderline personality disorder. About half of those with this disorder try suicide at least once, and the lifetime mortality rate from suicide among borderline personalities is an astonishing 10 per cent. Of course, these statistics should be treated with caution, for (as I noted above) suicidal behaviors are taken as symptomatic of borderline personality disorder. The second disorder is the eating disorder anorexia. One study found that anorexic individuals die from suicide at a rate 58 times higher than the general population.

Fortunately, borderline personality disorder and anorexia are uncommon disorders and are thus responsible for a comparatively small number of overall suicides. The disorders that play a role in the largest numbers of suicides are the mood disorders, namely major depression and bipolar disorder. A relatively small percentage of individuals with mood disorders (around 1 in 4) engage in suicidal behavior, and a smaller percentage actually die by suicide (a fact we will tackle later in this epilogue). But because the number of individuals who suffer from these disorders is large (in the tens of millions in the United States, for instance), these disorders serve to help explain a larger percentage of suicidal acts overall. Some researchers have concluded that 50-70 per cent of all suicidal individuals have a mood disorder. [1]

But even claiming that mental illness provides a motive for suicide does not capture the full truth of the matter. Mental illnesses are typically defined as conditions that persist through time. Depression, for instance, is defined not simply in terms of characteristic moods (such as sadness, worthlessness, or loss of interest or pleasure), but in terms of these characteristic moods persisting for at least two weeks. If depressed mood were a motive for suicidal behavior, we would expect that suicidal acts would, all other things being equal, occur at or near the onset of a depressive episode. But of course that is not the case, suggesting that though the mental illnesses that tend to produce suicidal thinking affect mood, suicidal behavior itself is triggered by more specific feelings that stem from, but are not simply symptomatic of, these mental illnesses.

So what are the specific feelings that trigger suicidal thinking and self-harming behavior? In choosing to end her life, an individual is not simply being pessimistic, thinking that the future is bleak. A suicidal person has gone beyond pessimism to a kind of nihilism, believing that her life is not worth living. Most research on the psychology of suicide echoes the idea that suicidal behavior is triggered by hopelessness. This hopelessness, again, stems not simply from the sense that the future looks difficult or challenging, but rather from the sense that the future looks dauntingly difficult or challenging and that there is no prospect that it could change. The suicidologist Thomas Joiner has concluded that this hopelessness nearly always contains two elements. The first is *perceived burdensomeness*. Suicidal individuals see themselves as incompetent or ineffective in a way that affects others:

> They perceive themselves to be ineffective or incompetent, but it's not just that. They also perceive that their ineffectiveness affects others, too. Finally, they perceive that this ineffectiveness that negatively affects others is stable and permanent, forcing a choice between continued perceptions of burdening others and escalating feelings of shame, on the one hand, or death on the other.[2]

Joiner is careful to emphasize that this burdensomeness is a matter of *perception*, not necessarily reality. Perhaps some suicidal people are, on balance,

---

1   The statistical summary in these paragraphs is drawn from K.R. Jamison, *Night Falls Fast: Understanding Suicide* (New York: Vintage, 2000), pp. 98-112.

2   *Why People Die by Suicide* (Cambridge, MA: Harvard University Press, 2007), p. 98.

burdensome to others, but what motivates suicidal behavior is merely the perception that one is burdensome to others. As a motive for suicidal behavior, perceived burdensomeness is in a way altruistic: the suicidal individual believes that others would be better off without her and so seeks to end her life in order to improve theirs.

The second element of suicidal hopelessness that Joiner identifies is *failed belongingness*. Suicidal individuals feel disconnected from others, as if they do not fully belong to any social group or to the human family generally speaking. They see themselves as isolated and peripheral to the world at large (and to the extent they are connected to that world, they are connected to it only insofar as they are burdensome to others). Joiner recounts a story of a suicidal man who left a note in his apartment, reading: "I'm going to the bridge. If one person smiles at me on the way, I will not jump."[1] This story vividly illustrates the profound need to belong or to be connected, and how, in this particular instance, the smallest indication of belonging or being connected can modify suicidal thinking.

Together, perceived burdensomeness and failed belongingness constitute what Joiner calls the typical "desire for death." We should of course be willing to acknowledge exceptions to Joiner's thesis (heroic suicides or suicides undertaken as acts of political protest, for example). But Joiner presents ample evidence that these two psychological factors make suicidal behavior, especially among the mentally ill, much more likely, and when such behavior does occur, the presence of these factors greatly shapes how lethal that behavior is.

Many suicides are highly solitary acts, taking place when a person is alone and outside of others' attention, yet Joiner's explanation of the psychological triggers of suicide reminds us that suicide is a highly social act despite being an anti-social act. The individual whose only perceived role in the larger community is to be a burden kills herself in order to exit a community for which, in her own eyes, she is not a functioning member.

The role of stressful events

One classic stereotype of a suicidal individual is the jilted lover: the man or woman who, having been rejected by his or her own true love, finds life unbearable and ends it, usually in a dramatic fashion (by drowning, self-immolation,

---

1   Joiner, p. 136.

or something similar), leaving behind a note that surpasses even the greatest poets in its insights into romantic love.

This is of course a stereotype, but it raises another key question about what causes suicidal behavior: the role of stressful life events. Do such events—job loss, divorce or separation, the death of a loved one, for example—play a role in causing suicidal behavior? Stressful events—even events that are positive stressors, such as recovery from an illness—have an impact on our thought patterns and how we deal with our moods and feelings. Most psychiatric research suggests that stressful events stimulate suicidal thinking because they worsen or intensify the symptoms of the mental disorders that are themselves associated with suicide. When individuals with mood disorders, for instance, experience stressful life events, their psyches tend to be more impacted than others and take longer to recover.

Here is an analogy that may shed insight on these phenomena. Individuals who have AIDS have compromised immune systems, since the AIDS virus attacks the cells that enable our bodies to fight disease. As a result, those with AIDS are far more susceptible to infectious illnesses that typically are not fatal for those who do not have AIDS. Indeed, those who die from AIDS do not really die of the disease as such; rather, they die from an infectious illness (for example, pneumonia) to which they would not ordinarily have been as vulnerable.

Stressful life events seem to operate on mentally ill people in the same way. Mental disorders "compromise" our emotional immune systems, magnifying the significance of stressful events. For instance, in mood disorders such as depression, an individual's mind is less psychologically malleable. A depressed person, for instance, is more likely to see losing her job as a reflection of her self-worth, as a permanent setback, and so forth. Unlike psychologically healthy individuals, she struggles to adapt to the stressful situation, and thus her depressive symptoms are exacerbated. In this respect, mental disorders make individuals more vulnerable to stresses, with the result that the disorders themselves worsen so as to make an already difficult course of life seem even worse. The psychologist Kay Redfield Jamison has elaborated this analogy:

> When the mind's flexibility and ability to adapt are undermined by mental illness, alcohol or drug abuse, or other psychiatric disorders, its defenses are put in jeopardy. Much as a compromised immune system is vulnerable to opportunistic infection, so too a diseased brain is made

assailable by the eventualities of life. The quickness and flexibility of a well mind, a belief or hope that things will eventually sort themselves out—these are the resources lost to a person whose brain is ill.[1]

Despite the plausibility of this analogy, there is still a danger in appealing to stressful life events to explain suicide. Such explanations are too linear. That his wife died, that she lost his job, that he learned he has cancer—these are convenient explanations for suicide, but they are far too simplistic. Plenty of psychologically resilient people manage the impact of stressful events and never come close to harming themselves in response. But mentally disordered persons are not so resilient, thus accounting for why even modest or ordinary stresses, such as disruptions in sleep patterns, seem to trigger suicidal acts on many occasions.

Means

Our discussion of motives nevertheless leaves us with a puzzle: a large number of people suffer from mental disorders such as depression and bipolar disorder, and a large number of people suffer from the particular feelings—thwarted belongingness and perceived burdensomeness—that are associated with suicidal ideation. But only a small number of those people try to kill themselves, and a smaller portion of those who try actually end up dying via acts of suicide. Therefore, it seems misguided to say that certain mental disorders or feelings of thwarted belongingness and perceived burdensomeness *cause* suicidal behavior. At most, these conditions often provide the background for suicidal behavior, but they are not by themselves its explanation. Mental disorders and feelings of hopelessness are at most necessary, but not sufficient, for suicidal behavior.

To identify the missing causal factor, consider a person who has both the motives of suicidal behavior identified above as well as an opportunity to end her life that answers to her motives and goals. What is left out of this picture? Obviously, a person must have the means to end her life, but the notion of having such a means is itself complex. As we discussed in Chapter Five, though suicidal people are often not especially choosy about the instruments

---

1   Jamison, p. 92.

they use to try to end their lives, denying people those instruments can nevertheless curtail the lethality of their suicide attempts. Hence, having a means that is perceived as suitable for suicidal behavior, regardless of its actual lethality, is necessary for a person to commit suicide. Furthermore, a suicidal person will not die unless she has the knowledge of how to use these means, probably a trivial matter in the case of a handgun, but less so in the case of ropes and poisons.

Still, there is an additional factor necessary to explain why acts of suicide occur. As noted above, many more people are mentally ill or psychologically disposed toward suicide than actually do it. Furthermore, many suicidal people report having had opportunities to end their lives that they did not take. So we are still left with the question of why some people are ultimately willing to opt for death and some are not. Here again, Joiner's recent research is relevant: he notes that the desire for suicide is much more common than is suicidal behavior itself. So what is different about those whose desire leads them to act and those whose desire does not? The innovation in Joiner's work arises from the simple proposition that suicide, the enacting of "lethal self-injury," is a learned behavior that people acquire through experiences of bodily injury or trauma. Death is fearsome, so in order to overcome the fear of death, a person must become accustomed to situations in which death is close at hand. Joiner's research indicates that individuals who are accustomed to such situations become increasingly comfortable with inflicting pain or violence upon themselves because the fear associated with pain or violence diminishes. As he puts it, suicidal individuals "habituate to self-injury" by being exposed to bodily harm and suffering.[1]

Joiner's hypothesis helps explain a wide body of data concerning suicidal behavior. First, it has long been recognized that past suicide attempts are the single greatest predictor of future suicide attempts. If Joiner's hypothesis is correct, this makes perfect sense: individuals become increasingly willing and able to harm themselves with each suicide attempt. Each subsequent attempt enables them to "learn" how to harm themselves more "successfully." Second, Joiner's hypothesis explains why, over individuals' lifetimes, their suicide attempts become more serious and lethal. Suicidal behavior becomes self-reinforcing, as individuals become less susceptible to pain and more accustomed to the prospect of death.

---

1 Joiner, p. 29.

Third, Joiner's hypothesis explains why people often seem to "work up to" suicide through acts of violence. Joiner uses the example of musician Kurt Cobain to illustrate this:

> Cobain was temperamentally fearful—afraid of needles, afraid of heights, and afraid of guns. Through repeated exposure and practice, a person initially afraid of heights, needles, and guns later became a daily self-injecting drug user, someone who climbed and dangled from thirty-foot scaffolding during concerts (at which times, incidentally, he would yell "I'm going to kill myself!"), and someone who enjoyed shooting guns. Regarding guns, Cobain initially thought they were barbaric and wanted nothing to do with them; later he agreed to go with his friend to shoot guns but would not get out of the car; on later excursions he got out of the car but would not touch the guns; and on still later trips, he agreed to let his friend show him how to aim and fire. Cobain died by a self-inflicted gunshot wound in 1994 at the age of twenty-seven.[1]

As Joiner observes, Cobain clearly worked up to suicidal behavior by familiarizing himself with instruments of self-injury.

Joiner's hypothesis also explains a common feeling among suicidal people: ambivalence about the prospect of their own death and a desire to be rescued. Until a person has been exposed to self-injury, they are almost certainly going to fear death and the pain they associate with killing themselves. Thus, even if a miserable person is otherwise psychologically disposed toward suicide, she may well be ambivalent or uncertain about wanting to die: her psychological suffering pulls her toward suicide, while her fear of pain or death pulls her away from suicide. That certain life experiences—for example, multiple surgeries, witnessing violence, drug abuse, accidents resulting in severe bodily trauma—are more common among suicidal people can also be explained by Joiner's hypothesis. Such experiences accustom the body to feeling or seeing pain or injury and would therefore eventually make suicide easier.

Finally, the relationship between a person's occupation and the likelihood of suicide is one of the most contested areas of suicide research. It is difficult enough to get reliable data about the prevalence of suicide, and still

---

1   Joiner, p. 51.

more difficult to gather evidence about the occupations of those who die by suicide. And ultimately it appears that a person's occupation has only modest power in predicting the likelihood of their being suicidal. Nevertheless, there is some evidence that police officers, members of the military, and physicians (especially dentists) are abnormally prone to suicide. If Joiner's hypothesis is correct, this is an unsurprising result, for all of these professions expose their practitioners to bodily harm, either to themselves or to other people. Police officers, members of the military, and physicians are therefore likely to become inured to bodily injury and more willing to inflict it upon themselves.

To date, I am not aware of a hypothesis besides Joiner's that so thoroughly explains why, among all those who consider suicide, only a handful end up trying it and still fewer end up dead from suicide. Of course, a more powerful hypothesis may be on the horizon, but Joiner's theories derive from a powerful but simple thought. Killing oneself is hard to do, requiring courage and fearlessness that few of us possess. There must, therefore, be characteristic processes by which those with the psychological profile associated with suicide (mental disorder, thwarted belongingness, and perceived burdensomeness) become actually suicidal. Joiner's novel suggestion is that among the necessary means of suicidal behavior is a willingness to engage in lethal self-injury, a willingness that is learned through repeated exposure to self-injury that makes a person more comfortable with pain or death. Once an individual has learned to be sufficiently comfortable or attracted to death, then suicidal behavior is increasingly likely.

* * *

In this epilogue, I have sought to identify the causes of suicidal behavior. As with any human behavioral phenomenon, this is not easy to do. But as a general answer, the one provided here seems plausible: suicidal behavior most often occurs when mentally ill individuals who have learned to subject themselves to self-injury and who are triggered by feelings of hopelessness have an opportunity to engage in suicidal behavior, an opportunity that reflects the goals and concerns motivating the behavior.

Of course, broad explanations are easier to find than explanations of why *particular* individuals try to take their own lives. As Jamison has put it:

> Each way to suicide is its own: intensely private, unknowable, and ter-
> rible. … [A]ny attempt by the living to chart this final terrain of life can
> be only a sketch, maddeningly incomplete.[1]

Suicide thus seems unfathomable and difficult for others to comprehend, even
with these broad explanations at hand. The act of suicide remains inscrutable
at its heart.

Further Reading

Jamison (2000) and Joiner (2007) both provide extensive discussion of the
causes of suicide. The American Association of Suicidology's website (http://
www.suicidology.org) also provides many resources about the origin of suicide. The late Edwin Shneidman (1918-2009) was widely considered the "dean"
of world suicidologists. His (1996) (1998), (1999), and (2004) books offer a
wealth of insights about the causes of suicide, as well as many illuminating
case studies.

---

1   Jamison, p. 73.

Conclusion and Summary

THIS SCOPE OF THE issues addressed in this book demonstrate that suicide is no simple matter, philosophically at least. The questions we have pursued are conceptual, epistemological, ethical, political, and psychological. My aim has been to give readers a foothold in the main philosophical issues surrounding suicide and to use the knowledge they acquire to investigate these issues further.

At the same time, I have defended a number of conclusions in this book, some of them controversial, others less so. Here are some of the main conclusions I have defended:

An adequate definition of suicide should be value neutral and at least capture the uncontroversial examples of acts that are (and are not) suicide. Defining suicide as intentional self-killing, regardless of its cause, appears to satisfy these requirements.

There is no generally sound argument that shows that suicide is always morally impermissible. Some secular arguments may show that it is morally impermissible on certain occasions.

Surprisingly, however, none of the most prominent arguments for the claim that suicide is always morally permissible is clearly sound either.

Although the notion of a duty to commit suicide is not incoherent, it is probably very rare.

There are defensible reasons to prevent, or intervene in, others' suicidal behavior, and such reasons stem from those individuals' own welfare and the tendency of suicidal thinking to flow from irrational patterns of thinking and feeling. Intervention and prevention efforts are more defensible, the better they respect individual autonomy and refrain from harm.

Whether we have a duty to aid others in their suicides depends on the moral justifiability of those suicides, our relationship to the individuals in question, and our competence in assisting.

A secondary goal of this book has been to illustrate how, even though suicide is an object of study for many disciplines, philosophy has a distinct contribution to make to our understanding of suicide. One of the most memorable recent literary treatments of suicide comes from Jeffrey Eugenides' novel *The Virgin Suicides*. The novel, told from the standpoint of a first-person plural narrator ("we"), describes the events leading up to the suicides of the five daughters in a well-to-do suburban family. As each Lisbon sister dies, a group of fascinated teenage boys collects objects that belonged to the girls (photographs, letters, and so on), in part to memorialize the girls but also in an effort to gain understanding about their lives. These objects take on a mystical or oracular quality:

> In the end we had the pieces of the puzzle, but no matter how we put them together, gaps remained, oddly shaped emptinesses mapped by what surrounded them, like countries we couldn't name. (Eugenides 2000: 241)

It would be vain to hope that a single book could solve the puzzle that is suicide. I will have accomplished my goal if our philosophical inquiry has given us reason to be optimistic that a solution is nearer at hand.

Bibliography

Alvarez, A. (1990). *The Savage God: A Study of Suicide*. New York: Bantam.

American Association of Suicidology. (2010). "National Suicide Stats and Tools." (http://www.suicidology.org/web/guest/stats-and-tools).

Aquinas, St. Thomas. (2007). *Summa Theologica*. Volume III, part II, second section. Trans. Fathers of the English Dominican Province. New York: Cosimo.

Augustine of Hippo. (1998). *City of God Against the Pagans*. Trans. B. Dombart and A. Kalb. Cambridge: Cambridge University Press.

Badcott, D. (2010). "Assisted dying: the influence of public opinion in an increasingly diverse society." *Medicine, Health Care, and Philosophy* 13: 389-97.

Baron, C.H. (2004). "Hastening death: the seven deadly sins of the status quo." In T.E. Quill and M.P. Battin (eds.), *Physician-Assisted Dying: The Case for Palliative Care and Patient Choice*. Baltimore: Johns Hopkins University Press. 309-22.

Battin, M. (1996). *The Death Debate. Ethical Issues in Suicide*. Upper Saddle River, NJ: Prentice-Hall.

—. (2005). *Ending Life: Ethics and the Way We Die*. Oxford: Oxford University Press.

Battin, M., R. Rhodes, and A. Silvers (eds.) (1998). *Physician-Assisted Suicide: Expanding the Debate*. New York: Routledge.

Battin, M., A. ven der Heide, L. Ganzini, G. van Der Wal, and B. Onwuteaka-Philipsen. (2007). "Legal physician-assisted dying in Oregon and the Netherlands: evidence concerning the impact on patients in 'vulnerable' groups." *Journal of Medical Ethics* 33: 591-97.

Baumrin, B. (1998). "Doctor, stay thy hand." In M.P. Battin, R. Rhodes, and A. Silvers (eds.), *Physician-Assisted Suicide: Expanding the Debate*. New York: Routledge. 177-81.

BBC World News America/Harris Poll. (2011). "Large Majorities Support Doctor Assisted Suicide for Terminally Ill Patients in Great Pain." (http://www.harrisinteractive.com/vault/HI-Harris-Poll-BBC-Doctor-Suicide-2011-01-25.pdf).

Beauchamp, T. (1992). "Suicide." In T. Regan (ed.), *Matters of Life and Death*. 3rd ed. New York: McGraw-Hill. 77-89.

Beck, A.T., M. Kovacs, and A. Weissman. (1979). "Assessment of suicidal intention: The Scale for Suicide Ideation." *Journal of Consulting and Clinical Psychology* 47: 343-52.

Benatar, D. (2008). *Better Never to Have Been*. Oxford: Oxford University Press.

Brandt, R. (1975). "The morality and rationality of suicide." In S. Perlin (ed.), *A Handbook for the Study of Suicide*. Oxford: Oxford University Press. 61-75.

Brody, B. (2010). *Suicide and Euthanasia: Historical and Contemporary Themes*. Dordrecht: Springer.

Brody, H. (2002). *Stories of Sickness*. 2nd ed. Oxford: Oxford University Press.

Callahan, D. (2005). "The case against euthanasia." In A. Cohen and C. Wellman (eds.), *Contemporary Debates in Applied Ethics*. New York: Blackwell. 179-90.

Camus, A. (1991). *The Myth of Sisyphus and Other Essays*. Trans. J. O'Brien. New York: Vintage.

Cholbi, M. (2000). "Kant and the irrationality of suicide." *History of Philosophy Quarterly* 17: 159-76.

—. (2002). "Suicide intervention and non-ideal Kantian theory." *Journal of Applied Philosophy* 19(3): 245-59.

—. (2007). "Self-manslaughter and the forensic classification of self-inflicted deaths." *Journal of Medical Ethics* 33: 155-57.

—. (2008). "Suicide." *Stanford Encyclopedia of Philosophy*. (http://plato.stanford.edu/entries/suicide/).

—. (2010). "The duty to die and the burdensomeness of living." *Bioethics* 24(8): 412-20.

Cicero. (1914). *De Finibus Bonorum et Malorum*. Trans. H. Rackham. London: William Heinemann.

Commission on the Study of Medical Practice Concerning Euthanasia. (1991). Medical Decisions about the End of Life, I. Report of the Committee to Study the Medical Practice Concerning Euthanasia. II. The Study for the Committee on Medical Practice Concerning Euthanasia. 2 vols. ["The Remmelink report."] The Hague: SdU.

Compassion in *Dying v. Washington*. (1994). 850 F. Supp. 1454.

Cosculluela, V. (1994). "The ethics of suicide prevention." *International Journal of Applied Philosophy* 9: 35-41.

—. (1995). *The Ethics of Suicide*. New York: Garland.

Cowley, C. (2006). "Suicide is neither rational nor irrational." *Ethical Theory and Moral Practice* 9(5): 495-504.

Devine, P.E. (1978). "On choosing death." *The Ethics of Homicide*. Ithaca, NY: Cornell University Press.

d'Holbach, Baron. (1970). *The System of Nature, or Laws of the Moral and Physical World.* Vol. 1. Trans. H.D. Robinson. New York: Burt Franklin.

Donnelly, J. (1998). *Suicide: Right or Wrong?* Amherst, NY: Prometheus Books.

Dresser, R. (1984). "Bound to treatment: the Ulysses contract." *Hastings Center Report* 14(3): 13-16.

Dworkin, G., R.G. Frey, and S. Bok. (1998). *Euthanasia and Physician-Assisted Suicide: For and Against*. Cambridge: Cambridge University Press.

Dworkin, R. (1993). *Life's Dominion*. New York: Knopf.

Dworkin, R., T. Nagel, R. Nozick, J. Rawls, and J.J. Thomson, et al. (1997). "Assisted suicide: The Philosophers' Brief." *New York Review of Books* 27 March. (http://www.nybooks.com/articles/archives/1997/mar/27/assisted-suicide-the-philosophers-brief/).

Eugenides, J. (2000). *The Virgin Suicides*. Eastsound, WA: Turtleback Press.

Fairbairn, G. (1995). *Contemplating Suicide: The Language and Ethics of Self-Harm*. New York: Routledge.

Feinberg, J. (1978). "Voluntary euthanasia and the inalienable right to life." *Philosophy and Public Affairs* 7 (2): 93-123.

Freud, S. (1961). *Beyond the Pleasure Principle*. Trans. J. Strachey. New York: Liveright.

Frey, R.G. (1998). "The fear of a slippery slope." In G. Dworkin, R.G. Frey, and S. Bok, *Euthanasia and Physician-Assisted Suicide: For and Against*. Cambridge: Cambridge University Press.

Gay-Williams, J. (2011). "The wrongfulness of euthanasia." In R. Munson (ed.), *Intervention and Reflection: Basic Issues in Medical Ethics*. 5th ed. Belmont, CA: Wadsworth. 168-71.

Glover, J. (1990). *Causing Death and Saving Lives*. Hammondsworth: Penguin.

Gorsuch, N. (2006). *The Future of Assisted Suicide and Euthanasia*. Princeton: Princeton University Press.

Graber, G. (1981). "The rationality of suicide." In S. Wallace and A. Eser (eds.), *Suicide and Euthanasia: The Rights of Personhood*. Knoxville: University of Tennessee Press. 51-65.

Grollman, E.A. (1988). *Suicide: Prevention, Intervention, Postvention*. Boston: Beacon
    Press.

Halpern, A., and G. Szmukler. (1997). "Psychiatric advance directives: reconciling
    autonomy and non-consensual treatment." *The Psychiatrist* 21: 323-27.

Hardwig, J. (1997a). "Dying at the right time—Reflections on assisted and unassisted
    suicide." In H. LaFollette (ed.), *Ethics in Practice*. New York: Blackwell. 48-59.

—. (1997b). "Is there a duty to die?" *Hastings Center Report* 27: 34-42.

—. (2000). *Is There a Duty to Die? and Other Essays in Bioethics*. New York: Routledge.

Holley, D.M. (1989). "Voluntary death, property rights, and the gift of life." *Journal of
    Religious Ethics* 17(1): 103-21.

Humber, J., and R. Almeder. (2000). *Is There a Duty to Die?* Totowa, NJ: Humana.

Hume, D. (1998). "Of suicide." In *Dialogues Concerning Natural Religion and Posthumous
    Essays*. Indianapolis: Hackett.

Hussain, T., and P. White. (2009). "GPs' views on the practice of physician-assisted suicide
    and their role in proposed UK legalisation: a qualitative study." *British Journal of
    General Practice* 59: 844-49.

Jamison, K.R. (2000). *Night Falls Fast: Understanding Suicide.* New York: Vintage.

Joiner, T. (2007). *Why People Die by Suicide*. Cambridge, MA: Harvard University Press.

Jones, J. (2001). "Transcript of Recovered FBI tape Q 42." The Jonestown Institute. (http://
    jonestown.sdsu.edu/AboutJonestown/Tapes/Tapes/DeathTape/Q042.html).

Kagan, S. (1989). *The Limits of Morality*. New York: Oxford University Press.

Kant, I. (1993). *Metaphysics of Morals*. Cambridge: Cambridge University Press.

Kapusta, N.D., E. Etzersdorfer, C. Krall, and G. Sonneck. (2007). "Firearm legislation
    reform in the European Union: impact on firearm availability, firearm suicide and
    homicide rates in Austria." *British Journal of Psychiatry* 191: 253-57.

Kupfer, J. (1990). "Suicide: its nature and moral evaluation." *Journal of Value Inquiry* 24:
    67-81.

Lee, W., A. Price, L. Rayner, and M. Hotpof. (2009). "Survey of doctors' opinions of the
    legalization of physician assisted suicide." *BMC Medical Ethics* 10:2. (http://www.
    biomedcentral.com/1472-6939/10/2).

Los Angeles Times. (2005). Editorial: "Planning for worse than taxes." 22 March. (http://
    articles.latimes.com/2005/mar/22/opinion/ed-wills22).

Luper, S. (2009). *Philosophy of Death*. Cambridge: Cambridge University Press.

McIntyre, A. (2009). "Doctrine of Double Effect." *Stanford Encyclopedia of Philosophy*.
    (http://plato.stanford.edu/entries/double-effect/).

Meier, D.E., C.A. Emmons, S. Wallenstein, T. Quill, R.S. Morrison, and C.K. Cassel. (1998). "A national survey of physician-assisted suicide and euthanasia in the United States." *New England Journal of Medicine* 338: 1193.

Mill, J.S. (1989). *On Liberty and Other Writings*. Cambridge: Cambridge University Press.

Minois, G. (1999). *History of Suicide: Voluntary Death in Western Culture*. Baltimore: Johns Hopkins Press.

Mishara, B. (2010). "Suicide types: rational suicide." In R. Kastenbaum (ed.), *Macmillan Encyclopedia of Death and Dying*. New York: Macmillan. 647-50.

Oregon Department of Human Services. (2009). "Death with Dignity Act annual reports." (http://www.oregon.gov/DHS/ph/pas/ar-index.shtml).

Parfit, D. (1987). *Reasons and Persons*. Oxford: Oxford University Press.

Perry, S. ("Sister Y") (2008). "An Introduction." View from Hell weblog. (http://theview-fromhell.blogspot.com/2008_03_01_archive.html).

ProCon.org. (2010). "International perspectives: legal status of euthanasia and assisted suicide." (http://euthanasia.procon.org/view.resource.php?resourceID=000136).

Raabe, P. (2002). *Issues in Philosophical Counseling*. Westport, CT: Prager.

Roberts, M., and D. Wasserman (eds.) (2009). *Harming Future Persons: Ethics, Genetics, and the Nonidentity Problem*. Dordrecht: Springer.

Schopenhauer, A. (1973). *Essays and Aphorisms*. New York: Penguin.

Seale, C. (2009). "Legalisation of euthanasia or physician-assisted suicide: survey of doctors' attitudes." *Palliative Medicine* 23: 205-12.

Seneca, Lucius Annaeus (Seneca the Younger) "On the Proper Time to Slip the Cable," in *Moral Epistles*. Trans. R.M. Gummere. The Loeb Classical Library. Cambridge, MA: Harvard University Press, 1917-25, volume 2.

Seymour, J.E., J. French, and E. Richardson. (2010). "Dying matters: Let's talk about it." *BMJ* 341: 4860.

Shneidman, E. (1996). *The Suicidal Mind*. Oxford: Oxford University Press.

—. (1998). *The Suicidal Mind*. Oxford: Oxford University Press.

—. (1999). *Lives and Deaths*. New York: Routledge.

—. (2004). *Autopsy of a Suicidal Mind*. Oxford: Oxford University Press.

Singer, P. (1994). *Rethinking Life and Death*. New York: St. Martin's.

—. (1997). "The drowning child and the expanding circle." *The New Internationalist* April 1997. (http://www.utilitarian.net/singer/by/199704—.htm).

Spellecy, R. (2003). "Revising Ulysses contracts." *Kennedy Institute of Ethics Journal* 13(4): 373-92.

Stern-Gillett, S. (1987). "The rhetoric of suicide." *Philosophy and Rhetoric* 20: 160-70.

Strunk, W., and E.B. White. (1995). *The Elements of Style*. 3rd ed. Boston: Allyn and Bacon.

Szasz, T. (1990). *The Untamed Tongue: A Dissenting Dictionary.* LaSalle, IL: Open Court.

van der Maas, P.J., J.I.M. van Delden, L. Pijnenborg, and C.W.N. Looman. (1991). "Euthanasia and other medical decisions concerning the end of life." *Lancet* 338: 669-74.

van der Maas, P.J., G. van der Wal, I. Haverkate, C.L. de Graaff, J.G. Kester, B.D. Onwuteaka-Philipsen, A. van der Heide, J.M. Bosma, and D.L. Willems. (1996). "Euthanasia, physician-assisted suicide, and other medical practices involving the end of life in the Netherlands, 1990-95." *New England Journal of Medicine* 335: 1699-1705.

Velleman, D. (1999). "A right of self-termination?" *Ethics* 109(3): 606-28.

—. (2008). "Beyond price." *Ethics* 118(2): 191-212.

Vyrostek, A., J.L. Annest, and G.W. Ryan. (2004). "Surveillance for fatal and nonfatal injuries—United States, 2001." *Morbidity and Mortality Weekly Report* 53 (SS07): 1-57 (http://www.cdc.gov/mmwr/preview/mmwrhtml/ss5307a1.htm).

Williams, B. (1972). *Morality.* Oxford: Oxford University Press.

Wittgenstein, L. (1979). *Notebooks: 1914-1916.* Trans G.H. von Wright and G.E.M. Anscombe. Chicago: University of Chicago Press.

Young, R. (2010). "Voluntary euthanasia." *Stanford Encyclopedia of Philosophy.* (http://plato.stanford.edu/entries/euthanasia-voluntary/).

Index